THE
HOROLOGICON

Praise for The Horologicon

'A magical new book ... Forsyth unveils a selection of obsolete, but oh-so-wonderful words'

Daily Mail

'If you love obscure words, then Mark Forsyth's *The Horologicon* will be for you.'

Daily Express

'*The Horologicon* lists many of the fabulous, obsolete gems of our language'

Carol Midgley, *The Times*

'This is surely the quirkiest, funniest English word book'

Good Book Guide

'Whether you are out on the pickaroon or ogo-pogoing for a bellibone, *The Horologicon* is a lexical lamppost.'

The Field

'Witty and entertaining ... [the] sheer enjoyment of words and deep study of them shines through every page.'

A Common Reader

'Reading *The Horologicon* in one sitting is very tempting'

Roland White, *Sunday Times*

'Forsyth serves up a feast of wonderful words to savour and cherish.'

Radio Times

'You should rush out to buy this ... a terrific book'

Theo Walden, *The Lady*

THE
HOROLOGICON

A Day's Jaunt
Through the Lost
Words of the English
Language

MARK FORSYTH

ICON

This edition published in the UK in 2013 by
Icon Books Ltd, Omnibus Business Centre,
39–41 North Road, London N7 9DP
email: info@iconbooks.net
www.iconbooks.net

Sold in the UK, Europe and Asia
by Faber & Faber Ltd, Bloomsbury House,
74–77 Great Russell Street,
London WC1B 3DA or their agents

Distributed in the UK, Europe and Asia
by TBS Ltd, TBS Distribution Centre, Colchester Road,
Frating Green, Colchester CO7 7DW

Distributed in Australia and New Zealand
by Allen & Unwin Pty Ltd,
PO Box 8500, 83 Alexander Street,
Crows Nest, NSW 2065

Distributed in South Africa by
Book Promotions, Office B4, The District,
41 Sir Lowry Road, Woodstock 7925

Distributed in Canada by Penguin Books Canada,
90 Eglinton Avenue East, Suite 700,
Toronto, Ontario M4P 2YE

ISBN: 978-184831-598-3

Typeset in Minion by Marie Doherty
Printed and bound in the UK by Clays Ltd, St Ives plc

Contents

About the author

Mark Forsyth is a writer, journalist, proof-reader, ghostwriter and pedant. He was given a copy of the *Oxford English Dictionary* as a christening present and has never looked back. In 2009 he started the Inky Fool blog, in order to share his heaps of useless information with a verbose world. He is also the author of the *Sunday Times* No. 1 bestseller *The Etymologicon*, published in 2011 by Icon Books.

The author would like to thank Jane Seeber and
Andrea Coleman for their judicious advice,
sensible suggestions and peculiar patience.

This book is the papery child of the Inky Fool blog, which was started in 2009. Though almost all the material is new, some of it has been adapted from its computerised parent. The blog is available at http://blog.inkyfool.com/ which is a part of the grander whole www.inkyfool.com.

Therefore doth Job open his mouth in vain;
he multiplieth words without knowledge.
Job 35, verse 16

For my parents

Preambulation

Tennyson once wrote that:

> Words, like Nature, half reveal
> And half conceal the soul within.

This book is firmly devoted to words of the latter half. It is for the words too beautiful to live long, too amusing to be taken seriously, too precise to become common, too vulgar to survive in polite society, or too poetic to thrive in this age of prose. They are a beautiful troupe hidden away in dusty dictionaries like *A glossary of words used in the wapentakes of Manley and Corringham, Lincolnshire* or the *Descriptive Dictionary and Atlas of Sexology* (a book that does actually contain maps). Of course, many of them are in the *Oxford English Dictionary* (OED), but not on the fashionable pages. They are the lost words, the great secrets of old civilisations that can still be useful to us today.

There are two reasons that these words are scattered and lost like atmic fragments. First, as already observed, they tend to hide in rather strange places. But even if you settle down and read both volumes of the *Dictionary of Obsolete and Provincial English* cover to cover (as I, for some reason, have) you will come across the problem of arrangement, which is obstinately alphabetical.

The problem with the alphabet is that it bears no relation to anything at all, and when words are arranged alphabetically they are uselessly separated. In the OED, for example, aardvarks are 19 volumes away from the zoo, yachts are 18 volumes from the beach, and wine is 17 volumes from the nearest corkscrew. One cannot simply say to oneself, 'I wonder whether there's a word for that' and turn to the dictionary. One chap did recently read the whole OED, but it took him a year, and if you tried that every time you were searching for the perfect word, you might return to find that the conversation had moved on.

The world is, I am told, speeding up. Everybody dashes around at a frightening pace, teleconferencing and speed-dating. They bounce around between meetings and brunches like so many coked-up pin-balls, and reading whole dictionaries is, for busy people like you, simply not feasible. Time is money, money is time, and these days nobody seems to have much of either.

Thus, as an honourable piece of public service, and as my own effort to revive the world's flagging economy through increased lexical efficiency, I have put together a Book of Hours, or *Horologicon*. In medieval times there were books of hours all over the place. They were filled with prayers so that, at any time of day, the pious priest could whip out his horologicon, flip to the appropriate page and offer up an orison to St Pantouffle, or whoever happened to be holy at the time. Similarly, my hope with this book is that it will be used as a work of speedy reference. 'What's the word?' you will think to yourself. Then you will check your watch, pull this book from its holster, turn to the appropriate page and find *ante-jentacular, gongoozler, bingo-mort*, or whatever it might be. This is a book of the words appropriate to each hour of the day. Importantly, as I have noted, it is a reference work. You should on no account attempt to read it cover to cover. If you do, Hell itself will hold no horrors for you, and neither the author nor his parent company will accept liability for any suicides, gun rampages or crazed nudity that may result.

Of course, there is a slight problem with attempting to create an efficient reference work of this kind, namely that I have to know what you are doing at every moment of the day. This isn't quite as hard as it sounds. I've consulted all of my friends and both of them have told me much the same story: they get up, they wash, they have breakfast and head off to work in an office. Neither of them is quite clear what they do there, but they insist that it's important and involves meetings and phone calls, work-shy subordinates and unruly bosses. Then they pop to the shops, eat supper and, as often as not, head out for a drink. It is on this basis that I have made a game attempt at guessing your hypothetical life.

Some things I have, quite deliberately, ignored. For example, there are no children because they are much too unpredictable. I have included a chapter on courtship for reasons explained at the time. I haven't quite been able to decide whether you are married – sometimes you are and sometimes you aren't – although I am sure that you must possess a firmer opinion. Throughout, I have taken the liberty of imagining you as being half as lazy, dishonest and gluttonous as I am. You have to write about what you know. If you are a piece of virtue into whose wipe-clean mind sin and negligence have never entered, I apologise. This is not the book for you and I hope you have kept the receipt. And of course the nature of your job is a bit of a mystery and a sticking point.

Though most of this is being written in the British Library, as that is where the dictionaries are, the British Library is in fact very like an office, except that nobody is allowed to talk. It has all the usual usualnesses – i.e. the lady on my left has spent the last hour on Facebook, occasionally chortling quietly – and it has all the usual eccentricities – i.e. the chap on my right has all sorts of behemothic tomes on the theories of post-Marxist historiography out on his desk, but is in fact reading *Sharpe's Revenge* under the table, and thinks nobody has noticed.

I mean, I assume you work in an office, but I suppose I may be wrong. Though I have drawn on all the knowledge I could, I can never be quite sure that I've got you down to a T. You might not work in an office at all. You might be a surgeon, or a pilot, or a cattle rustler, or an assassin, taking a little break between hits to find out the lost gems and *hapax legomena* of the English language before heading out for a hard day's garrotting.

You could do anything, anything at all. Your life might be a constant welter of obscenity and strangeness. For all I know, you could spend all day inserting live eels into a horse's bottom. If you do, I must apologise for the arrangement of this book, and the only consolation I can offer is that there is a single eighteenth-century English word for shoving live eels up a horse's arse. Here is the definition given in Captain Grose's *Dictionary of the Vulgar Tongue*:

> **FEAGUE.** To feague a horse; to put ginger up a horse's fundament, and formerly, as it is said, a live eel, to make him lively and carry his tail well; it is said, a forfeit is incurred by any horse-dealer's servant, who shall show a horse without first feaguing him. Feague is used, figuratively, for encouraging or spiriting one up.

There are three instructive points to be taken from that

definition. First, you should never trust an eighteenth-century horse dealer. Especially if you're a horse. Or an eel.

Second, the English language is ready for anything. If you were to surprise a Frenchman in the act of putting a conger up a mare's bottom he would probably have to splutter his way through several sentences of circumlocutory verbocination. However, ask an English-speaker why they are sodomising a horse with a creature from the deep and they can simply raise a casual eyebrow and ask: 'Can't you see I'm feaguing?'

The ability to explain why you're putting an eel up a horse with such holophrastic precision is the birthright of every English-speaking man and woman, and we must reclaim it.

Thirdly, and finally, you will notice that that definition is not from the *Oxford English Dictionary*. Though the OED is the greatest and heaviest reference work yet devised by man, it does not necessarily touch the sides of the English language. In the case of feaguing, the OED does actually quote Grose, but rather coyly mentions only the stuff about ginger. Other words have been grabbed from rural dialects and criminals' dens. Any dictionary that I could find, I have used; from Cab Calloway's *Hepsters Dictionary: Language of Jive* (1944) all the way back to the rainswept miseries of Old English. I shall probably slap together a list of all the works used and stick it at the back, just in case anybody reads that far.

If I have found a word in a dictionary, any dictionary, then it has merited inclusion. Wise and learned professors have asked what makes a word truly a word. I neither know nor care. Such questions I leave to my betters. I must be content to tootle my lexicographic kazoo and dance my antic hay near, but not in, the sacred grove of Academe.

Chapter 1

6 a.m. – Dawn

*Alarm clocks – trying to get back to sleep
– feigning illness*

∽∼∾

There is a single Old English word meaning 'lying awake before dawn and worrying'. *Uhtceare* is not a well-known word even by Old English standards, which were pretty damn low. In fact, there is only one recorded instance of it actually being used. But uhtceare is there in the dictionaries nonetheless, still awake and waiting for dawn.

Uht (pronounced *oot*) is the restless hour before the dawn, when Aurora herself is loitering somewhere below the eastern horizon, rosying up her fingers and getting ready for the day. But for now, it is dark. And in the *antelucan* hush you should be happily slumbering and dreaming of pretty things.

If you are not, if you are lying there with your eyes wide open glaring at the ceiling, you are probably suffering from a severe case of uhtceare.

There's an old saying that the darkest hour comes just before the dawn. However, that's utter tosh. If you get out of bed and peek through the window, you will see a pale glow in the east. But don't, whatever you do, actually get out of bed. It's probably chilly and you'll never get your posture in bed (technically called your *decubitus*) quite right again. You'll just have to lie there and try not think about how horrid it all is.

Ceare (pronounced *key-are-a*) was the Old English word for care and sorrow, emotions that have an annoying habit of striking during the uht. For some reason these early hours are the time when you remember all your sins and unpaid bills and, perhaps, the indelicate thing you did last night, and as each of these creeps into your mind your uhtceare grows more and more severe.

For an affliction so common, uhtceare is a very rare word. It is recorded only once in a poem called *The Wife's Lament*, which, surprisingly, isn't about how awful and messy her husband is, but about how he has been exiled to a far country and left her here with her uhtceare and her vicious in-laws. Old English poetry is almost universally miserable, and Old English poets should really have bucked up a bit, but they did give us *uhtceare* and for that we should be grateful.

The Old English used to cure their uhtceare by going to listen to the monks singing their uht song. But the monks are long since gone and you have nothing to distract you except for the possible chirruping of an insomniac songbird or the gentle sound of the dustman.

One qualification remains, though, before you self-diagnose with uhtceare. Are you sure you're awake?

Many is the time that I have lain awake before dawn thinking that I would be able to get back to sleep if only this giant squirrel would stop chasing me round the dentist's surgery. These strange half-dreamful, half-conscious delusions and illusions have a technical name – they are *hypnopompic*. *Hypno* from the Greek for sleep and *pompic* from the word for sending.

Nor should you be too keenly *oneirocritical*. Oneirocritical means 'of or pertaining to the interpretation of dreams'. If your dream has a meaning it is probably obscene, and best forgotten, something that will happen in a couple of minutes anyway.

So best to suffer your uhtceare in silence and wait for the *day-raw*, which is the first streak of red in the dawn sky. Aside from being terribly pretty and a warning to shepherds, the day-raw will also decide whether today is a *high* or *low dawn*. Low dawn is when the sun appears straight over the horizon, high dawn is when it is, at first, obscured by clouds and then pops out suddenly in its glorious nuclear-fusive majesty farther up in the sky.

Whatever happens, this is the *dayening*, the *greking*. An eighteenth-century highwayman would have called it the *lightmans*, for some reason, and would probably have decided that this was the time to go home to bed, making way for the eighteenth-century farmers who would have called it, rather charmingly, the *day-peep*. Exhausted chorus girls in 1940s New York would have called it *early bright*. But for you it is simply the end of your usual uhtceare and the cue, one suspects, for your *expergefactor*.

Alarm clocks

An expergefactor is anything that wakes you up. This may simply be your alarm clock, in which case it is time to hit the snooze button. But it may be a dustman or a milkman or a delivery van, in which case it is time to lean out of your window and shriek: 'Damn you all, you expergefactors!' This ought to keep them quiet until one of them has at least found a good dictionary.

You may, though, not have opted for the alarm clock. Many people, for reasons that baffle, make the radio their expergefactor of choice. If this is the case, you will be horribly awoken by news of far-off massacres, earthquakes, plagues, elections etc., or by voices of anxious politicians explaining exactly why they were utterly blameless and how the money or mistress was simply resting in their account or bed.

The technical term for a dishonest politician is a *snollygoster*. Well, all right, it may not be the technical term, but it is the best one. The OED defines *snollygoster* as 'A shrewd, unprincipled person, esp. a politician', although an American journalist of the 1890s defined it more precisely (if less clearly) as:

> … a fellow who wants office, regardless of party, platform or principles, and who, whenever he wins, gets there by the sheer force of monumental talknophical assumnacy.

Unfortunately, the American journalist didn't stop to explain what *talknophical* or *assumnacy* meant. I can't see why snollygoster has fallen out of use, unless perhaps politicians have all become honest, in which case the rest of us owe them an apology.

If you feel that snollygoster is too ridiculous a way to refer to a dishonest man who holds public office, you may always refer to that voice on the radio by the name *throttlebottom*.

Either way, you shouldn't use the radio news as a means to wake you up, as it is liable to irritate or depress or both. Also it may distract you from the correct method of expergefaction: an *aubade*.

Turn off the radio.

Turn off the alarm clock.

Listen carefully.

Do you hear an aubade?

An aubade is a song sung at dawn by your lover beneath your bedroom window. Providing that your lover can carry a tune, a good aubade is enough to put you in a merry mood until at least breakfast. However, if you cannot, at present, hear an aubade there are only two sad possibilities: I am sorry to have to break this to you so early in the day, but either your lover is a lazy, *lollygagging* shirker of his/her duties; or you have no lover at all.

In the olden days they had a much better system of waking people up. There was a chap called a *knocker-up* who would wander around the village tapping on people's bedroom windows with a special stick. This was actually considered a proper job and was probably a lot safer than its alternative: the *weaver's larum*.

A weaver's larum was an odd device that worked like this. Take a reasonably heavy object like a stone or a small child and tie two pieces of string to it. Both these pieces of string should then be fed through a single hook. One of them should be attached to the wall, so that the string is taut and the stone/baby dangles. The second piece of string, which is loose, should be tied to your finger.

Got that? Heavy object attached by a taut string to the wall and by a loose string to your finger.

Right, now get a tall, thin candle and put its base right next to the taut bit of string. Now light the candle and drift off to sleep. During the night the candle will slowly burn down and down until the flame gets to the piece of string, which is incinerated.

The stone/baby falls to the floor and your finger gets a vigorous yank to pull you rudely from your slumbers.

The final possibility is a *reveille*. This is the drum roll or bugle-blast that's meant to waken a whole barracks full of soldiers. It's thus a term that can usefully be applied to the noise of dustmen, children or any of the other inconveniences and natural expergefactors of modern life.

Zwodder

Uhtceare is now officially over; however, that does not mean that you feel great. There is a word for people who are breezy and bright in the morning: *matutinal*. In fact, there are a bunch of words, but most of them are rude. As Oscar Wilde observed, only dull people are brilliant at breakfast. And, anyway, breakfast is still a long way off.

For the moment, you can lie there in a *zwodder* cursing the arrival of a new day. The rather racy lexicographical classic *Observations on some of the Dialects in the West of England, particularly Somersetshire* (1825) defines a zwodder as: 'A drowsy and stupid state of body or mind.'

This would, in and of itself, make zwodder a useful word. But the really important thing is how it sounds. Say it. *Zwodder*. It's the sort of word that can and should be mumbled from the refuge of your bedclothes. *Zwodder*. It's the drowsiest word in the English language, but there's also something warm and comfortable about it.

Alternatively, you could be addled, stupefied and generally speaking *philogrobolized*, a word that should be said at about an octave beneath your normal speaking voice and reserved for the morning after the carnage before. As responses to 'How are you this morning?' go, 'Philogrobolized' is almost unbeatable. Nobody will ever have to ask you what you mean as it's all somehow contained in the syllable *grob*, which is where the stress should always be laid. It conveys a hangover, without ever having to admit that you've been drinking.

Another rather more religious way of doing this is to speak enigmatically of your *ale-passion*. Passion here is being used in its old sense of suffering, as in the Passion of Christ. (That a word for suffering became a synonym for romantic love tells you all you need to know about romance.) Ale-passion is mentioned in the 1593 book *Bacchus Bountie* in the following context:

> Fourthly, came wallowing in a German, borne in Mentz, his name was Gotfrey Grouthead; with him he brought a wallet full of woodcocks heads; the braines thereof, tempered with other sauce, is a passing preseruatiue against the ale-passion, or paine in the pate.

In fact, you should probably keep a small aviary of woodcocks next to your bed, just in case. If not, you will lie there feeling awful. You will suffer from *xerostomia*, the proper medical term for dryness of the mouth through lack of saliva. But there will be nothing you can do about it unless you actually get out of bed. You're also liable to have slumbered in the wrong decubitus and found that your arm has fallen asleep, a condition that the medical world refers to as *obdormition*. The only way to cure this is to wave the said limb about frantically, like a string-puppet having a fit, until the *prinkling* starts and your blood slowly, reluctantly resumes its patrol.

Alas that such sufferings should invade your bleary-eyed *lippitude*. Now is the zwoddery time when you wish that you'd invested in thicker curtains, for the sun is insistent, and you are one of those *lucifugous* creatures that avoids sunlight like a vampire, or a badger. Lucifugous (or light-fleeing) is a word that is usually applied to sins and demons, but it can just as well refer to somebody making a tactical retreat beneath the duvet because they cannot endure the gaze of heaven.

The final suffering of dawn is *pissuprest*. A horse-keeper's manual from 1610 says: 'Pissuprest in a horse, is when a horse would faine stale, but cannot.'

And that's you, comfortable in your covers, with this *micturition*, this intense desire to urinate, that can only be relieved if you actually get out of bed and stumble to the lavatory. But not yet, not yet. All my possessions (as Queen Elizabeth almost said) for one more moment in bed. Perhaps if you lie here the micturition will magically vanish.

It is time for procrastination and *cunctation* and generally putting off the inevitable. There's nothing wrong with that. This is, after all, life in miniature. We know that death and going to the lavatory are inevitable, but that doesn't mean we have to do it cheerfully or leap enthusiastically into the grave. Hold out! Enjoy the brief moment that you have. Treasure and savour your *grufeling*, which is defined in *Jamieson's Etymological Dictionary of the Scottish Language* (1825) thus:

To be grufeling: To lie close wrapped up, and in a comfortable-looking manner; used in ridicule.

The Scots are clearly a nation devoid of pity, or indeed of medical knowledge. Don't they realise that you may be suffering from undiagnosed *dysania*? Dysania is extreme difficulty in waking up and getting out of bed, and there may be a secret epidemic of it.

Slightly better known is *clinomania*, which is an obsessive desire to lie down. But that doesn't quite answer, does it? Perhaps you'd be better off with Dr Johnson's word *oscitancy*, which he defined as 'Yawning or unusual sleepiness'. The first recorded usage of the word back in 1610 mentions 'such oscitancie and gaping drowsiness' in describing the effects of a dull sermon in church. You can accompany your oscitation with *pandiculation*, which is the stretching of the arms and body characteristic of this mournful yawnful time.

If you were king in the dawns of old, this would be the moment to hold your *levee*. A levee was a funny sort of formal occasion when you would lie in bed while all your social inferiors came to congratulate you on your superiority. Unfortunately the system of levees got out of hand in the eighteenth century. There were so many of them, and so many degrees of society, that those at the top were forced to remain in bed until early afternoon. The novelist Henry Fielding described it thus in 1742:

> … early in the morning arises the postillion, or some other boy, which no great families, no more than great ships, are without, and falls to brushing the clothes and cleaning the shoes of John the footman; who, being drest himself, applies his hands to the same labours for Mr Second-hand, the squire's gentleman; the gentleman in the like manner, a little later in the day, attends the squire; the squire is no sooner equipped than he attends

the levee of my lord; which is no sooner over than my lord himself is seen at the levee of the favourite, who, after the hour of homage is at an end, appears himself to pay homage to the levee of his sovereign. Nor is there, perhaps, in this whole ladder of dependance, any one step at a greater distance from the other than the first from the second; so that to a philosopher the question might only seem, whether you would chuse to be a great man at six in the morning, or at two in the afternoon.

During a levee you should know that your favourite courtiers are allowed to stand in the *ruelle*, which is the space between the bed and the wall where your shoes and socks are probably lying. Everybody else must make do with milling around at the foot of the bed or even by the door.

If you are conducting a levee, I wish you well. But these days the closest thing to a levee is the early-morning phone call to your boss to *egrote*.

Egrote is a fantastically useful word meaning 'to feign sickness in order to avoid work'. If it has fallen out of use, the cause must be that workers have lost their cunning. So here are some instructions for a beginner.

Wait until your boss has answered the phone and then start to *whindle*. Whindling is defined in a dictionary of 1699 as 'feigned groaning'. It's vital to whindle for a while before giving your name in a weak voice. Explain that you are a *sickrel* and that work is beyond you. If asked for details, say that you're *floccilating* (feverishly plucking at the bedclothes) and *jactating* (tossing around feverishly).

If your boss insists that you name your actual condition, don't call it dysania. Go instead for a severe case of *hum durgeon*. Unless your boss is fluent in eighteenth-century slang he'll never suspect that:

> **HUM DURGEON**. An imaginary illness. He has got the hum durgeon, the thickest part of his thigh is nearest his arse; i.e. nothing ails him except low spirits.

Unfortunately, you cannot use hum durgeon every day. Your employer will suspect. You can probably get away with it at most twice a week, and the second time you should probably just shriek 'My thighs! My thighs!' down the telephone until they hang up.

No. You have been lying here too long and too languorously. Seven o'clock is upon us. Throw off the duvet! Toss away the sheet! And crawl out of bed.

Chapter 2

7 a.m. – Waking and Washing

Slippers – looking in the mirror – self-loathing – lavatory – shower – hair – shaving – brushing your teeth

～～～

Exodus

That's it. You're out of bed. Like Adam and Eve expelled from Eden.

First, grope for your slippers, or to give them their much merrier name: *pantofles*. Pantofles are named after Saint Pantouffle who is as obscure as he is fictional. He (or she, or it) appears to have been invented in France in the fifteenth century. Nobody knows why the French would have invented a saint, or indeed why slippers should be named after him, but they were and that's that. Robert Burton's great medical work *The Anatomy of Melancholy* describes how Venus, the goddess of love, was so enraged with her blind son Cupid making people fall in love willy-nilly that:

> ... she threatened to break his bow and arrows, to clip his wings, and whipped him besides on the bare buttocks with her pantophle.

And any slipper that can double up as a weapon with which to spank godlings has to be a good idea.

Once your toes are snugly pantofled, you can stagger off to the bathroom, pausing only to look at the little depression that you have left in your bed, the dip where you have been lying all night. This is known as a *staddle*.

The bathroom

Part I: The looking glass and what you saw there

There are a lot of synonyms for mirror – everything from *tooting-glass* (Elizabethan) to *rum-peeper* (eighteenth-century highwayman), but the best is probably the *considering glass*. That is, after all, what you do with the thing. But first, before you even peek in the considering glass, take a *gowpen* of water – i.e. a double handful – and throw it over your face. After all, nobody but an angel is beautiful before eight o'clock.

The word *pimginnit* may be necessary here. It's a seventeenth-century term meaning 'a large, red, angry pimple'. This is a particularly fine definition as it implies that pimples have emotions, and that some of them are furious. Pimginnits are much more wrathful than, for example, *grog-blossoms*, which are those spots that pop up the morning after one has indulged in too much grog, or rum. Grog-blossoms are more sullen than angry, like a resentful letter mailed overnight from your liver.

But enough of your *furuncles*. Let us just say that you are *erumpent*, which is a jolly-sounding way of saying spotty (nicer than *papuliferous* and infinitely more pleasant than *petechial*, a word that Dr Johnson defined as 'pestilentially spotted'). There are too many other sorrows for us to get hung up on spots.

First, there are the *elf-locks*. It is, or was, a well known fact that elves sneak into your bedroom during the night with no better motive than to tangle up your hair. The sad result, which you will see reflected, is elf-locks.

Then there are the wrinkles and, in extreme cases, *wrines* (these are the big ones); the crows' feet, the *frumples*, the *frounces*, the lurking *lirks* and a million other synonyms for the lines on your face, which are, after all, merely signs of how thoughtful and wise you are.

There's also the *culf*, which is the name for the bed fluff that has lodged in your navel. There are the red *ferret-eyes* through which you're looking. There's the *ozostomia* and *bromodrosis*, which is what a doctor would call your stinking breath and sweat, because doctors have a lovely habit of insulting you in Greek, which softens the blow. Almost anything sounds softer in a classical language. For example, if a fellow were to suggest that you stank of horse piss, you would probably take offence, but if he merely said that you were *jumentous*, you might imagine that the chap was telling you that you were *jubilant* and *momentous*, or something along those lines. You might even thank him.

All in all, though, you are *idiorepulsive* (you disgust even yourself) and something really ought be done about it soon. However, I fear that things must get worse before they can get better.

On particularly bad mornings, this may be the time to attempt a *through cough*. These aren't easy. I have tried it myself and consistently failed. If you can cough and fart at precisely the same instant then you have achieved what was known – two hundred years ago – as a through cough, and can therefore continue the rest of the day with a feeling of secret satisfaction.

Anyway, a through cough is only the preface to the lowest part of the day – that part when you are no better than a beast and no worse than a monarch: the lavatory.

Part II: The Spice Islands

In the Book of Samuel, as the whole history and future of salvation is being worked out between Saul and David, everything comes to rest upon Saul's popping to the lavatory. Not, of course, that they had proper lavatories in those days. Salvation was not that far advanced. But as Saul with his army hunted for David beside the Dead Sea, he found that his dinner was, like his kingship of Israel, a fleeting thing that he would be forced to relinquish.

> Then Saul took three thousand chosen men out of all Israel, and went to seek David and his men upon the rocks of the wild goat. And he came to the sheepcotes by the way, where was a cave; and Saul went in to cover his feet: and David and his men remained in the sides of the cave. And the men of David said unto him, Behold the day of which the LORD said unto thee, Behold I will deliver thine enemy into thine hand, that thou mayest do to him as it shall seem good unto thee. Then David arose, and cut off the skirt of Saul's robe privily.

What concerns us here is not the question of who was truly the Lord's anointed, nor the symbolism of the king's cloak, nor even the necessity of checking your lavatory carefully for rival claimants to the throne; but the delightful phrase *to cover his feet*, which is a literal rendering of the ancient Hebrew meaning to do the necessities of nature.

If the Bible teaches us one thing, it's that you should never be so vulgar as to call a spade a spade or a lavatory a lavatory. Even if you choose not to cover your feet (which should already have pantofles on them), you can disguise your baseness with all sorts of lovely phrases. The Victorians would visit *Mrs Jones*, or *my aunt*, or *the coffee shop*, although that last phrase may be too suggestive for those of a liquid disposition. Others have been more exotic. In the thirteenth century they would visit *a chamber foreign*, or in the eighteenth century you could take *a voyage to the Spice Islands*, these being the most exotic place imaginable, and particularly appropriate for the morning after a curry.

However, these references to exoticism may be inappropriate to something that is often so troubling in foreign lands. The great actor David Garrick took a trip to Europe in 1764 and wrote to his brother saying:

> ... I never, since I left England, till now, have regal'd Myself with a good house of Office, or as he calls it, a *Conveniency* – the holes in Germany are generally too large, & too round, chiefly owing I believe to the broader bottoms of the Germans [...] We have a little English Gentleman with us who Slipt up to the Middle of one of the holes & we were some Minutes before we could disengage him. – in short you may assure Townley, (Who loves to hear of the state of these Matters) that in Italy the People *do their Needs*, in Germany they *disEmbogue*, but in England (& in England only) they *Ease* themselves.

House of office has a pleasing grandeur to it, although some of Garrick's contemporaries would have called it a *House of Commons*, which is good for the politically-minded. Medieval fellows would *go to siege*, which has a fine martial ring and is particularly appropriate for the constipated. And militarism was still present in the Victorian *scraping castle*. In fact, there are a million and one variants and euphemisms, all of which mean that since the thirteenth century nobody has had to be so vulgar as to *do their filth-hood*.

While actually on the *gong-hole* one should take care about one's precise actions. For example, in a house with thin walls it is a little rude to *squitter* or 'void the excrement with a noise'. Your *purgation*, *exoneration*, *dejection* or whatever you choose to call it should be performed pianissimo and the *tantadlin tart* baked in silence.

When it is all over you may turn your attention to the necessary paperwork, and if you think that the English language may fail you here, then you haven't read Sir Thomas Urquhart's 1653 translation of Rabelais, which has this tantalising little tip:

> I say and maintain, that of all torcheculs, arsewisps, bumfodders, tail-napkins, bunghole cleansers, and wipe-breeches, there is none in the world comparable to the neck of a goose, that is well downed, if you hold her head betwixt your legs. And believe me therein upon mine honour, for you will thereby feel in your nockhole a most wonderful pleasure, both in regard of the softness of the said down and of the temperate heat of the goose …

Bumfodder has had a rather curious history in the English language, for though it is now a very obscure word for loo roll, it still survives in a shortened form. *Bumf* is, to this day, a rather derogatory term for large, but necessary, amounts of paperwork. And necessary it certainly is, if you want to avoid what were once called *fartleberries*.

However, in the dire circumstance that you have neither paper nor a back-up goose, you can always resort to a corner of your cloak, provided David hasn't crept up on you and cut it off, privily.

Part III: For all the water in the ocean/Can never turn the swan's black legs to white,/Although she lave them hourly in the flood

Benjamin Franklin invented the lightning conductor, bifocal glasses, the chair-desk and the *cold air bath*. This last innovation he described in a letter of 1768. The crux of it was that he didn't like water:

> The shock of the cold water has always appeared to me, generally speaking, as too violent, and I have found it much more agreeable to my constitution to bathe in another element, I mean cold air. With this view I rise almost every morning, and sit in my chamber without any clothes whatever, half an hour or an hour, according to the season, either reading or writing.

In the interests of water conservation, Franklin's invention could be usefully revived, although it is hard to see what effect it would have on dirt and smell. So we of the twenty-first century are probably stuck with water; and, such is the pressure of time, we are probably going to use a shower. The best thing about taking a bath is that you get to use the 1950s American slang term *make like a fish*.

However, before launching rashly into the waters, you should prepare. Sod's Law states that you'll be halfway through showering before you realise that there's almost no shampoo left in the bottle; so you should *duffifie* it now. Duffifie is an old Aberdeenshire verb meaning 'to lay a bottle on its side for some time ... that it may be completely drained of the few drops remaining'. It's therefore much more compact than the English equivalent of *making the bottle confess*. Either way, a bit of duffifying will save you much annoyance later on.

As you set the waters running you might wish to notice the *shower curtain effect*, which would doubtless have interested Benjamin Franklin. When the shower starts, the curtain will be sucked in towards you, and though several theories have been proposed, modern science is still uncertain as to why this happens.

Even as the curtains are being pulled in around you, you will probably experience the *curglaff*, which is another old Scots term, this time for the feeling you get when you're hit with cold water. Your heart gallops, your blood rushes, and, if you're Benjamin Franklin, you don't like it one little bit.

Anyway, there's nothing to be done about that. It is time to *buddle* (scrub in water) all that is not *illutible* (unwash-awayable). Baudelaire said that humans were deluded if they thought they could wash away all their spots with vile tears, but Baudelaire was French and therefore knew nothing about hygiene or shower gel.

There are funny words for almost all the parts of the body, but the important ones in the shower are these:

Oxter – armpit

Popliteal – behind the knees

Dew-beaters/beetle-crushers – feet (depending on your usual use for them)

Inguinal – relating to the groin

Everywhere else is optional. After all, if you spend too long in there you'll end up with the skin on the ends of your fingers *quobbled*.

Part IV: Stare, stare in the basin/And wonder what you've missed

Hair

The Scots used to have a terrible reputation for lice. Whether this was justified, I don't know. I deal in dictionaries, not Scotsmen. However, *the Scots Greys are in full march* once meant that lice were crawling all over your head. And a dictionary of 1811 defines *clan* thus:

> A family's tribe or brotherhood; a word much used in Scotland. The head of the clan; the chief: an allusion to a story of a Scotchman, who, when a very large louse crept down his arm, put him back again, saying he was the head of the clan, and that, if injured, all the rest would resent it.

All of which should explain why a comb used to be called a *Scotch louse trap*. So reviving this term will enrich the language and enrage the Scots, which is a double benefit.

In fact, one can continue to enrage the Celtic fringes of the hair by dispensing with your comb and instead using your fingers to get your hair into some semblance of order. The Welsh had no reputation for lice, but they did once have a reputation for using cheap substitutes. So a *Welsh diamond* is a crystal, a *Welsh carpet* is a pattern painted on the floor, and a *Welsh comb* is your five fingers.

The things people do to their hair are so weird and varied that the English language is brimming with useful words on the subject, most of which contain the element *trich-*, which was the ancient Greek word for the stuff. For example, smooth-haired people are *lissotrichous* and wavy-haired people are *cymotrichous*, and *trichotillomania* is a manic desire to pull out all your hair.

If dictionaries are to be believed then the best possible thing you can do is cultivate dangling curls. Even Dr Johnson's dictionary called a woman's curls *heart-breakers*, and the Victorians called them *bow-catchers*, on the basis that they would catch handsome young men, or *beaus*. And Victorian women, in a rare fit of equality, would run after men who sported *bell-ropes*, which brought *belles* to ruin with their curly charms.

Shaving

Let us now turn our attention to the chins of men and unfortunate ladies. Let us turn to *shavery*, which the OED solemnly defines as 'subjection to the necessity of being shaved', although the poet Robert Southey used it better when he observed in 1838:

> Oh pitiable condition of human kind! One colour is born to slavery abroad, and one sex to shavery at home! – A woman to secure her comfort and well-being in this country stands in need of one thing only, which is a good husband; but a

man has to provide himself with two things, a good wife, and a good razor, and it is more difficult to find the latter than the former.

Slavery has been abolished but shavery survives. This latter is rather a shame, as it lessens the need for all of the technical beard words, of which there are many. They all involve the Greek root *pogo*, which is pronounced in exactly the same way as the stick (although the two are etymologically unrelated). So there's *pogonology* (the study of beards), *pogonate* (having a beard), *pogoniasis* (a beard on a lady), and *pogonotomy* (shaving). As we live in an essentially misopogonistic society of beard-haters, most men must start the day by taking a razor from the *pogonion* or tip of the chin up to the *philtrum*, which is the name for the little groove between your nose and your upper lip. Then you have to work carefully to avoid a neckbeard, which the Victorians called a *Newgate fringe*. Newgate was the name of a London prison where people were hanged. So a Newgate fringe was meant to resemble the rope that was slipped around the felon's neck before he took the plunge into eternity.

Teeth

In the first century BC, the Roman poet Catullus wrote these lines about a man called Aemilius:

Non (ita me di ament) quicquam referre putaui,
utrumne os an culum olfacerem Aemilio.
Nilo mundius hoc, niloque immundius illud,
uerum etiam culus mundior et melior:
nam sine dentibus hic.

It is impossible to capture the solemn beauty of the original in English, but a loose translation might go:

> I really cannot tell between
> His mouth above and arse beneath;
> They are identically unclean,
> The only difference: one has teeth.

Nothing else is known about filthy-breathed Aemilius beyond Catullus's poem. For two thousand years that has been his sole posterity. From this we may learn two lessons: don't get on the wrong side of poets, and keep your teeth clean.[1]

So open your mouth wide and say *oze*. It's a lovely, long, wide-throated word and means 'a stench in the mouth'. The good thing about oze is that merely by saying it, you distribute it.

When toothpaste manufacturers talk about the small amount of toothpaste that fits on the end of your toothbrush, they call it a *nurdle*. Why they should do so is lost in the oze of time, but it's been the word since at least 1968, and a recent court case between two of the largest manufacturers was centred entirely around who was allowed to depict which nurdle on their packaging. Not only was the nurdle said to chase away oze, it could also whiten your teeth (or, to be more technical about it, stop your being *xanthodontic*).

However, the greatest advance since the days of Catullus is the introduction of mouthwash, which was, unfortunately,

---

[1] In fact, Catullus wrote another poem about a chap with shiny white teeth, claiming that they only got that way because he drank piss. There's no pleasing some poets.

introduced after the words *squiggle* and *gleek* had died out. Squiggle was an old Norfolk dialect word meaning 'to shake and wash a fluid about in the mouth, with the lips closed'. Squiggling is a lovely word because it sounds exactly like what it is, as does gleek. To gleek is to squirt liquid from your mouth. This should be done from as far from the basin as possible, just for the challenge.

Done

That's it. You're done. There may be other things you should take care of, but I'm much too shy to enquire. Instead, I shall ask what God asked your forebears in the garden of Eden: Who told you you were naked?

Chapter 3

8 a.m. – Dressing and Breakfast

Clothes – make-up – breakfast – preparing to depart

༄༅༅

Naturism is all very well, but it gets chilly after a while. So it is time to become what nudists refer to as a *textile*, i.e. one of those poor fools who wears clothes. You're ready to get togged up, to become the *concinnate* (finely dressed) and consummate gentleman; or if you are of the womanly persuasion, to become a *dandizette*, the nineteenth-century term for a female dandy. Certainly you cannot remain starkers or, as a witch would put it, *sky-clad*.

In the second century AD a group of Christian fanatics called Adamites practised Adamism, or holy nudity, but only in church, and even there they had to have central heating. St Epiphanius described Adamism thus:

> Their churches are stoves, made warm for the reception of company by a fire underneath. When they come to the door they pull off their clothes, both men and women, and enter naked in to the place of meeting. Their presidents and teachers do the same, and they sit together promiscuously. And so they perform their readings and other parts of worship naked.

The theory of Adamism, if you can believe it, was that by expos-
ing themselves to such temptation they actually strengthened
their wills and conquered lust. But though God may have
approved of the Adamites (He has remained silent on the subject), the police and most employers take a dim view. So let us
dress.

We begin with what the Victorians coyly referred to as one's
abbreviations, which in these coarse times is simply called under-
wear. In Herefordshire, capacious and roomy knickers used to
be known as *apple-catchers* on the basis that they were large
enough to serve a useful purpose in a late-summer orchard.

Moving to other unmentionables, the English language is
weirdly wanting in slang terms for the brassiere. The only fun to
be had is with padded bras, which were known in the 1940s as
gay deceivers. As you can imagine, this was before the word gay
had become widely used as slang for homosexual, and when a
gay old man could still be lusting after members of the opposite
sex. Such gays could be deceived by the use of rubber falsities,
which, because pure rubber is a trifle smelly, would be flavoured
with chocolate. It might be worthwhile to bring back the gay old
terminology, but not the technology.

There's a curious little entry in *A New Dictionary of the Terms
Ancient and Modern of the Canting Crew* (1699):

> **Sir Posthumus Hobby**, one who Draws on his Breeches with a
> Shoeing-horn, also a Fellow that is Nice and Whimsical in the
> set of his Cloaths.

It's curious for two reasons. First, it doesn't mention whether
the shoeing-horn is necessary because the fellow is fat, or

because he wears terribly tight trousers to show off his lovely legs. Secondly, there really was a chap called Sir Posthumus Hoby who had lived a hundred years before that dictionary was written. He was a famous Puritan and may well have been the model for the stern and strict Malvolio in Shakespeare's *Twelfth Night*. But that Sir Posthumus (so named because he was born after his father's death) was neither particularly fat nor particularly dandyish. Indeed, the only really notable things about him were his humourlessness and the fact that he matriculated at Oxford at the age of eight. Nonetheless, it seems unfair to deny him immortality at that awkward moment when you try to slip into the clothes of last year's slimness.

It is at this point that you're bound to notice a *grinnow*. A grinnow is a stain that has not come out in the wash and that you probably haven't seen until this vital moment. For a word that useful, it's astonishing that grinnow is only recorded as an obscure Shropshire dialect word in a dictionary of 1879, where they provide the helpful sample sentence: 'I canna get the grinnows out if I rub the piece out, they'n bin biled in so many times.'

One must be wary of grinnows; too many grinnows and you end up looking like a *tatterdemalion*. A tatterdemalion is a chap (or chappess) whose clothes are tattered and torn. It is the same as a *tatter-wallop*, a *ragabash*, or a *flabergudgion*; and, given the threadbare state of modern fashion, it is an eminently useful word.

Tatterdemalion has the lovely suggestion of dandelions towards the end (although pronounced with all the stress on the *may* of malion) and should be immediately comprehensible even to the uninitiated, because everybody knows what *tatter* means, and the *demalion* bit was never anything more than a linguistic fascinator. More wonderfully still, there are spin-off words: *tatterdemalionism* and *tatterdemalionry*, the latter meaning tatterdemalions considered as a group.

Once you are *snogly geared* (as they said in the eighteenth century), *dressed to death* (nineteenth century) or simply *togged to the bricks* (twentieth-century Harlem), it is time, if you are a lady, to apply some auxiliary beauty.

Make-up

Everybody remembers the line 'Alas, poor Yorick', but fewer recall the final lines of Hamlet's skull speech. 'Now get you to my lady's chamber, and tell her, let her paint an inch thick, to this favour she must come; make her laugh at that.' Which shows that Hamlet was not the sort of person to help you choose a lipstick.

It is tempting to bring back all the winsome words that Shakespeare would have known for make-up. In his time there would have been no brutal application of foundation, as ladies would *surfle* instead. They would then apply *ceruse* as a blusher, the eyes would have been touched with *collyrium* and the eyelids with *calliblephary*. But as the whole process back then was called *fucation*, it's probably best not to get carried away with Elizabethan vocabulary. It could become awkward if your husband called, 'What's taking so long?' and you accidentally replied: 'I just need to fucate, darling. Won't be a minute.' To which your significant other might reasonably reply: 'Eight?'

So we must content ourselves with a few 1940s terms for auxiliary beauty such as *pucker paint* for lipstick. The 1940s also provide the splendid phrase *preparing bait*, which takes in the whole process of lustrification. It imagines the prinked paintress and perfumeress as a fisherlady, her lips as the hooks, and men as mere fish.

The *ante-jentacular* part of the day is almost over. Ante-jentacular is simply an immensely clever-sounding adjective meaning 'before breakfast'. It is best applied to strenuous exercise or Bloody Marys.

Breakfast

The Greek for breakfast was *ariston*, so the study of breakfast is *aristology*, and those who devote their lives to the pursuit of the perfect morning meal are *aristologists*. The subject had a brief vogue in the mid-nineteenth century and there was even a book published called *Cookery for the Many*, by *an Australian Aristologist*; but it is now a forgotten art. This is a shame, as breakfast presents a wide buffet to the enquiring mind. Who but an aristologist would be able to tell you that a *ben joltram* was 'brown bread soaked in skimmed milk; the usual breakfast of ploughboys', that a *butter shag* was 'a slice of bread and butter', or that *opsony* was strictly defined in the OED as 'any food eaten with bread' (plural: *opsonia*).

The disciplined student of aristology must begin their studies nearly three millennia ago with Homer, as there is a whole book of the *Iliad* – the nineteenth – devoted to the subject of whether or not to eat breakfast.

Essentially, Agamemnon gives a long speech commanding the Greeks to *jenticulate* (which is the posh way of saying eat your breakfast). Achilles, though, is having none of it and gives an even longer speech pointing out that they are late for work (i.e. killing Trojans) and really ought to get on with it. Odysseus then weighs in with an even longer speech that essentially says, 'It's the most important meal of the day. You may not feel like it now, but when you're bathing in the blood of your enemies you'll regret it.' Achilles says that really, he'd rather not, especially as his breakfast always used to be made by his best friend Patroclus, whose mangled body now lies in his tent with its feet towards the door. He then turns to the corpse and gives a rather lovely little speech that goes:

> 'Thou,' said he, 'when this speed was pursued
> Against the Trojans, evermore apposedst in my tent
> A pleasing breakfast; being so free, and sweetly diligent,
> Thou madest all meat sweet.'

And that would have been that, except that the gods themselves are very keen that Achilles should have a hearty breakfast, so, at Zeus's direct order, Athena descends from heaven and magically instils 'heaven's most-to-be-desired feast' directly into his body, thus allowing him to set off to work. Then there's a brief incident with a talking horse and the book ends.

Had Achilles been a more reasonable man he might have settled for a quick *chota hazri*, which is a brief breakfast that is just enough to keep you going till elevenses. The term comes from the British empire in India and is simply Hindi for 'little breakfast', but it has much more history and glamour to it than that. It's the sort of snack that you eat after spending the night up a tree with a tiger. So, when a chap in 1886 did just that, he returned at dawn and:

> … he was hailed by his friends amid a perfect shower of ejaculations; all the answer they got was a wail of hunger and a cry for 'chota hazri,' after which Brown promised to relate his adventures faithfully and truly.

It reminds one of the sort of world where a gobbled energy bar or brief banana was not an indignity, it was simply something that you wolfed down because you were in a hurry to conquer the earth.

If you have time on your hands and a hole in your stomach you can cook yourself a proper breakfast, not quite as proper as 'heaven's most-to-be-desired feast', but a damned good second place. Achilles, for example, would never have seen a chicken or a hen's egg, as they weren't imported to Europe until the fifth century BC. So familiar are eggs to us, however, that in the eighteenth century they were referred to as *cackling farts*, on the basis that chickens cackled all the time and eggs came out of the back of them. Unlike Achilles, we can have them fried, boiled, scrambled, coddled, poached, devilled, Benedict or Florentine.

A much grander eggy word is *vitelline*, which means 'of or pertaining to egg yolk'. The seventeenth-century poet Robert Herrick once wrote:

> Fain would I kiss my Julia's dainty leg,
> Which is as white and hairless as an egg.

Which shows an unsettling erotic fascination with breakfast, and also misses the point that though egg whites sustain you, it is the vitelline parts that yield the true glory. It is the vitelline yumminess into which you can dip what Mr Herrick's contemporaries would have called *ruff peck*, which to us is merely a rasher of bacon.

The earliest explanation for why it's called a rasher comes from John Minsheu's *Ductor in Linguas* of 1612 where he explains that it gets 'rashly or hastily roasted'. Modern etymologists are much less fun and think rasher relates vaguely to razor. Nonetheless, a rashly roasted rasher can easily end up *brizzled*, or 'scorched near to burning'. Brizzled is a lovely word, onomatopoeic of the sound that pigmeat will make as it burns and sizzles its way to deliciousness.

All of this can be washed down with a glass of *yarrum* (thieves' slang for milk), or, if you are feeling rakish, a *whet*, an early-morning glass of white wine, popular in the eighteenth century but terribly hard to find in these drier and duller days. In fact, in the Age of Enlightenment they would often breakfast on a thing called *conny wabble*, which was 'eggs and brandy beat up together', although sadly no more precise recipe than that survives.

In fact, there are an almost infinite number of possible breakfasts and this brief book cannot contain them all. One would need a seasoned aristologist to look into all the nooks and crannies. For example, there was once such a thing as a *Spitalfields breakfast* that crops up in a dictionary of Victorian slang:

> **Spitalfields breakfast**, at the East end of London this is understood as consisting of a tight necktie and a short pipe.

Which I assume means dressing hurriedly and valuing tobacco over food. If you go further back through the slang dictionaries things get more gruesome. Back in the seventeenth and eighteenth centuries, when the death penalty was punishment for almost anything (this is before the invention of Australia and deportation), there were a million and one artful phrases and euphemisms for being hanged. You could *dance upon nothing with a hempen cravat* or *caper in the wind* or, if the hanging were at dawn you could:

> Have a hearty choke and caper sauce for breakfast – To be hanged

There was even a euphemism for this euphemism, mentioned in an article of 1841 called *Flowers of Hemp; or the Newgate Garland*. The author is searching for a particular criminal and is told by an informant that:

> 'He died last Wednesday morning of a vegetable breakfast, that did not altogether agree with his digestive system.'
>
> 'A vegetable breakfast! What do you mean?'
>
> 'Mean! well now, the like of that! And so you do not perceive, that this is what Dr Lardner calls a delicate form of expression for "a hearty choke with caper sauce."'
>
> 'As we live and learn, sir; I am much beholden to you for the information,' I replied, hardly able to repress my disgust at the brutal jocularity of the wretch.

So it's worthwhile remembering as you sweep the crumbs from the table that it could all be a lot worse.

Once upon a time, back in ancient Greece, they had a special slave called an *analecta* whose job was to gather up the breadcrumbs after a meal. *Ana* meant 'up' and *lectos* meant 'gathered'. That's why the gathered up sayings of Confucius are called *The Analects*, and that's also why Henry Cockerham's *English Dictionarie* of 1623 has the entry:

Analects, crums which fall from the table.

Conge

A *conge* (pronounced *kon-jee*) is a formal preparation to depart. It's the sort of thing medieval kings did before processing around their kingdom or that beautiful princesses performed before being shipped off to marry a distant emperor. However, conges today tend to be much more disorganised affairs as you realise that you're running late, haven't got your phone, haven't charged your phone, can't find your car keys and have forgotten to put on your trousers. You are much more likely to end up running around in circles (or *circumgyrating* as Dr Johnson would have put it). The conge of today consists of grabbing everything that you possibly can into an *oxter lift*, an old Scots term for as much as you can carry between your arm and your side.

Now charge for the door, and with a quick cry of 'Abyssinia' (which was the hepcat way of saying 'I'll be seein' ya'), you are off to work.

Chapter 4

9 a.m. – Commute

Weather – transport – car – bus – train – arriving late

◦∽᷈᷈∾◦

The weather

When a death sentence is commuted to life imprisonment, it's a good thing. However, commuting is uniformly awful. The connection between them, since you ask, is that both involve a *commutual* exchange. The noose is exchanged for the cell, small debts can be commuted for one large debt, and in nineteenth-century America individual purchases of railway tickets could be exchanged for one *commutation ticket* at a slightly reduced rate, that was valid for a year.

However, you are still at your front door. It is said that every journey begins with a single step, but in my experience, every journey begins with a single step followed by a disorderly retreat once I realise that I'm sporting the wrong clothes for the weather or have forgotten my wallet or hipflask or crossbow. So let us begin with a *celivagous* (or 'heavenward-wandering') glance.

The worst form of weather is a *pogonip*, which is a word we stole from the Shoshone Indians (along with the rest of their possessions) to describe a fog so cold that it freezes into ice crystals in mid-air. Actual pogonips are quite rare, as air needs to get down to about −40°C before the water in it crystallises, but reality should never get in the way of talking about the weather. Real pogonips tend to be very localised affairs, occurring in deep Alaskan valleys and the like, so you can always claim that there was a sudden pogonip on your street, and nobody will be any the wiser.

Non-Alaskan commuters are much more likely to find the weather *swale*. Swale is recorded in the indispensable *A Collection of English Words, not generally used* (1674), where it is defined as:

Swale: windy, cold, bleak.

It barely needs to be mentioned that swale is a north-country word, but nor do you even really need the definition. Swale is already a windy, cold, bleak word. It sways between *wail* and *windswept*, and is irresistibly suggestive of rain, misery and Yorkshire.

And more miserable even than the skies of northern England are the skies of Scotland, where they actually have the word *thwankin*, which is dismally defined in a dour dictionary of Scots as:

Thwankin: used of clouds, mingling in thick and gloomy succession.

If it is swale and the clouds are thwankin, you should probably turn back and grab your umbrella. But no! Etymologically speaking, an umbrella is something that shades you. The Latin for shade is *umbra*, and *ella* is just a diminutive. So *umbrella* is 'a little shade' – the same as a *parasol* or 'defence against the sun' – and as the clouds are already thwankin and swale you'll need a *bumbershoot*.

A bumbershoot is exactly the same as an umbrella, but it's a much better word. The *bumber* bit is a variant of brolly, and the *shoot* is there because it looks a little bit like a parachute. Bumbershoot is first recorded in America in the 1890s and, for some reason, never made it across the Atlantic, which is a crying shame as it's a beautiful word to say aloud.

If you have no bumbershoot, you will have to make do with a *Golgotha*, which was the Victorian slang term for a hat, on the basis that, as it says in Mark's Gospel:

> And they bring him unto the place Golgotha, which is, being interpreted, The place of a skull.

So with a Golgotha on your head, and bumbershoot in hand, you may now *hurple* onwards, hurple being a verb defined in an 1862 glossary of Leeds dialect as:

> To shrug up the neck and creep along the streets with a shivering sensation of cold, as an ill-clad person may do on a winter's morning. 'Goas hurpling abart fit to give a body t'dithers to luke at him!'

However, there remains the possibility that you open the door to discover that the skies are blue, the sun has got his Golgotha on, and it's a lovely day. This is unlikely, especially in Leeds, but possible. If it is a hot day, then the English language allows you to use almost any word beginning with the letters SW. *Sweltering*, *swoly*, *swolten*, *swole-hot*, *swullocking*, *swallocky* will all do; however, it should be noted that swallocky means that a thunderstorm is on the way, so you should still have your bumbershoot to hand.

The very best sort of morning, though, is the *cobweb morning*. This is an old Norfolk term for the kind of morning when all the cobwebs are spangled with dew and gleaming in the misty hedgerows. On such mornings, when the world is *dewbediamonded*, you can almost forgive your expergefactor for waking you and your work for compelling you out from your house. Dew is a beautiful thing, often said to be the tears of Aurora, goddess of the dawn, although what she's crying about is never specified. If you are of a scientific bent, you can measure dew using a *drosometer*. If you are of a poetic bent, you can contemplate what Browning called the 'sweet dew silence'. If you are of a practical bent, you can worry about getting your feet wet, for morning moisture can have calamitous consequences, such as *beau traps*.

Have you ever trodden upon an innocent-looking paving stone, only to find that there is a hidden hole full of water beneath it? The stone tilts down under your weight and the disgusting dirty rainwater (once known as *dog's soup*) spurts up all over your ankles and into your shoes. There is a name for this. It is called a beau trap, on the basis that it destroys the leggings of the finely dressed beau about town. Grose's *Dictionary of the Vulgar Tongue* from 1811 demonstrates that some annoyances are eternal:

Beau Trap A loose stone in a pavement, under which water lodges, and on being trod upon, squirts it up, to the great

damage of white stockings; also a sharper neatly dressed, lying
in wait for raw country squires, or ignorant fops.

And the worst possible consequence of a beau trap is to have
your shoes filled with water so that you can actually hear it
sloshing and squeezing between your toes. There is a word for
making this noise: *chorking*, as in this Scots poem of 1721:

Aft have I wid thro' glens with chorking feet,
When neither plaid nor kelt cou'd fend the weet.[1]

In fact, it may be best to set off to work on *scatches*, which are
defined in a dictionary of 1721 as stilts to put the feet in to walk
in dirty places, and it would certainly show a sense of balance
and altitude that would make you the envy of your neighbours.
Also, scatches would allow ladies to be sure that their skirts were
never *daggled*, which is to say muddied at the hemline. However,
walking on scatches would, I imagine, require an awful lot of
practice and they would be hard to stow away at work, so you
could instead go for *backsters*, which are the planks of wood laid
out over soft mud used by people who want to wander around
on the seashore without getting their boots or their clothes dirty.

That's it. The door has closed behind you. So it's time to check
whether you've got your keys and your phone and your purse or
wallet. This is done by *grubbling* in your pockets. Grubbling is
like groping, except less organised. It is a verb that usually refers
to pockets, but can also be used for feeling around in desk draw-
ers that are filled with nicknacks and whatnot. It can even have a

---

[1] Scots dialect was invented by poets who couldn't think of a rhyme.

non-pocket-related sexual sense, although this is rare and seems only ever to have been used by the poet Dryden, as in his translation of Ovid's *Ars Amatoria* where he rather wistfully arranges to meet his lover thus:

> There I will be, and there we cannot miss,
> Perhaps to Grubble, or at least to Kiss.

Having established beyond doubt that you've forgotten your keys, that your wallet/purse is empty and that your phone is not charged, you can now decide that it's too late to do anything about it and instead *incede* (advance majestically) to work. Or, if inceding is beyond you, you may *trampoose* to your chosen mode of transport.

Transport

There are so many methods of getting to and from your place of labour that the lexicographically-minded may simply drown in words. Pliny the Elder records that in the days of Augustus Caesar a boy managed to train a dolphin to carry him to school every morning, a story that resulted in the English word *delphinestrian*. However, in default of a dolphin you may make do with a *cacolet*, which is a comfortable basket affixed to a mule for the benefit of Pyrenean travellers. You could even *brachiate* to work, brachiate being the technical term for the way that Tarzan swings through the jungle. This gives a fantastic workout to the upper body, but requires that you have a continuous line of trees between your house and your office. If you have enough horses and too little sleep, you could opt for a *besage*, which is a bed carried on the backs of four horses. I would say that a besage was the finest form of transport that I've ever heard of, except that I can't see how the horses would know which way to go if their passenger were snoozing. And it's a cruel thing to put somebody in a bed and not allow them to sleep. If there was a solution to this problem of the besage, it is not, alas, recorded in the *Dictionary of Obsolete and Provincial English*.

Cars

But to return to the more prosaic methods of transport, let us begin with the motorcar. In the Second Book of Kings, God decides that he doesn't like Ahab one little bit. In fact, he wants to 'cut off from Ahab him that pisseth against the wall'. This is actually a relatively common ancient Hebrew phrase meaning 'every man jack of them'. Anyway, the chosen instrument of God's off-cutting will be a chap called Jehu (pronounced *gee who*). So Jehu jumps into a chariot and heads off to kill the king. The king's watchman sees the approaching chariot and dashes down to tell the monarch that 'the driving is like the driving of Jehu son of Nimshi; for he driveth furiously.' This one clause in the Bible was all that the English language needed to import his name and immortalise Jehu as a noun for a furious driver.

A *jehu* is a particularly bad (or good) thing if you are driving down *jumblegut lane*, which was an eighteenth-century term for a bumpy road too obvious in its origin to require any explanation at all. However, jehus and jumbleguts aside, you are much more likely to get caught in a *thrombosis* of traffic, wherein the veiny and arterial roads of the metropolis are blocked by the embolism of roadworks and by clots that have broken down.

Thus Jehu sits immobile in his chariot and gazes enviously at
the bus lane.

Bus

The plural of bus is, of course, *buses*. But it's a curious little
point of history that, etymologically, the plural of bus would
be *bus*. The *voiture omnibus*, or 'carriage for everybody' was
introduced in Paris in 1820, and the plural would be *voitures
omnibus*, which wouldn't affect the shortening at all. (The same,
incidentally, would apply to the *taximeter cabriolet*.)

The central problem with buses is that you wait for ages and
then none come along. This waiting (or *prestolating*) is a miserable affair as it's usually raining, and you huddle up in the bus
shelter, which starts to feel rather like a *xenodochium* or hostel
for pilgrims, inhabited by people who peer optimistically down
the road for the approaching Godot.

When your bus does arrive, it is all too likely to be *chiliander*,
or containing a thousand men, at which point you have to bar-
rel onto the monkey board like a spermatozoa trying to get into
the egg. Once within, you have no choice but to *scrouge*, which
is helpfully defined in the OED thus:

> To incommode by pressing against (a person); to encroach on
> (a person's) space in sitting or standing; to crowd. Also, to push
> or squeeze (a thing).

But scrouge you must, and furiously, while at the same time
looking out for *chariot buzzers*. Chariot buzzers are pickpockets
who work on buses, but as the term is Victorian, you ought to be
able to recognise them by their antiquated attire.

Margaret Thatcher never said 'Anybody seen in a bus over the age of thirty has been a failure in life.' However, the poet Brian Howard (1905–58) did. It's a rather snobby-sounding comment, but given that Brian Howard published only one serious book of poems, and given that the one biography of him is titled *Portrait of a Failure*, one must assume that he spent a lot of time on buses himself.

Nonetheless, the over-thirty-year-old who wishes to be thought a success, but has no access to an automobile or jetpack, should probably opt for a sub- or superterranean train.

Train

Trains present their own problems. For starters you need to fight your way singlehanded through a railway station just to get on one. This involves dodging a lot people with heavy, bruising suitcases who are all milling around like an illustration of Brownian motion.

The people who design guided missiles refer to a *balladromic course*, which is the path that a rocket takes towards its target, ignoring everything else and moving at speeds in excess of Mach 3. This is probably the best way to approach a station concourse: know where your platform is and be ready to explode at the slightest provocation. Keep it balladromic.

If you are of a more pacifist and peacenik disposition, you could always *gaincope*, which is 'to go across a field the nearest way', and is a word more suited to the pastures and meadows of Olde Englande. But what you really need is a *whiffler*.

There are very few whifflers today, if any; and I've never understood this, as a whiffler for hire at a station entrance could make an awful lot of money during rush hour. A whiffler is, according to the OED:

> One of a body of attendants armed with a javelin, battle-axe, sword, or staff, and wearing a chain, employed to keep the way clear for a procession.

Of course, a full-time whiffler (if you could afford one) would be useful at all sorts of events such as Christmas shopping or cocktail parties. But at rush hour, a whiffler is not merely useful, but necessary. Without your whiffler you may well be reduced to a state of *hemothymia*, which is what psychiatrists call an impulse to murder, or, more literally, bloodlust.

If you are ever reduced to such a helpless state of violent anger that you want to set about your fellow commuters with a bow and arrow, you should be comforted that the English language already has a phrase in place for you. Grose's *Dictionary of the Vulgar Tongue* (1811) says:

> **Have among you, you blind harpers**; an expression used in throwing or shooting at random among the crowd.

This constitutes some usefully enigmatic final words before the ticket inspector wrestles you to the ground.

If you ever do make it to the train, then you can settle down with your coffee and newspaper and spend your journey chuckling over the obituaries. Incidentally, the thing round the coffee cup that stops you burning your fingers is a *zarf*, and a newspaper is much more fun when referred to as a *scream sheet*.

None of this applies of course if the train is so *thringed*, thronged and crammed that you cannot get a seat. Whether this is better or worse than being scrouged in a bus or clotted in a traffic thrombosis is a question that I cannot answer; all I can tell you is that the standard unit of measurement for pain is a *dol* and is measured with a *dolorimeter*.

Clocking in

By the time you arrive anywhere near your place of work you ought to be exhausted, bruised, battered, frustrated and generally broken in to twenty-first-century life. Nothing from here on in can be as bad as the commute, so things are looking up. You may celebrate this fact with a sly *dew drink*, which is a beer taken before the working day begins. This will delay you still further, but as you are almost inevitably the *postreme* (one who is last) as it stands, and as your tardiness is hardly your fault but can be blamed on the traffic/trains/bus driver/vengeful God or whatnot, a dew drink seems to be exactly what you need and deserve.

Once refreshed you can stride into the *barracoon*, or slave depot, refreshed and ready to do a passable impression of a day's work. Of course, you don't stride into the barracoon: the correct method for entering the workplace is to *scuddle* in, which Dr Johnson defined as:

Scuddle: To run with a kind of affected haste or precipitation.

It doesn't matter how slowly you ambled up the front steps. Or how you paused to admire the pretty clouds in the sky: the actual entrance to the office should be done at a scuddle. The correct method is to hyperventilate a few times to make yourself out of breath. Once gasping, give both cheeks a firm pinch and then hurl yourself at the doors, slamming them loudly as you shoot through and stagger to a halt in the middle of your office. Try to speak. You can't. You're too out of breath, swallowing air like a man who has nearly drowned. At last, gazing around you with wild innocent eyes, and with your scuddle complete, you finally manage to ask with perfect seeming-sincerity, and as though you don't already know the answer to the question: 'Am I late?'

Chapter 5

10 a.m. – The Morning Meeting

*Staying awake – listening – arguing – yes, no, who cares?
– mugwumps – keeping quiet*

ﾟﾟﾟ

Offices are peculiar places and nobody is ever quite sure what happens in them, least of all the people who work there. But the day tends to begin with a morning meeting, in which everybody decides what they will fail to do for the rest of the day. This is usually held around a little table, or, in a particularly modern office, standing up or even walking, a strangely nomadic habit known as *pedeconferencing*. Indeed, if trends continue, the offices of the future will hold their morning meetings at an all-out sprint, with the winner getting to be boss for the day.

Medieval guilds would call this a *morn-speech*, the ancient Greeks a *panegyris*, the medieval church a *synod*. In Turkey a council of state was called a *divan*, after which the item of furniture is named – so in Milton's *Paradise Lost*, when all the demons of Hell are 'rais'd from their dark divan', it has nothing to do with comfy seating arrangements. However, the best word for a meeting is a *latrocinium*.

A latrocinium is, technically speaking, a robber-council. So, when deciding what to thieve next, Ali Baba and his 40 thieves would have held a 41-strong latrocinium in their magical cave. It is up to the conscience of the individual office-worker to decide whether it is a latrocinium that they attend, but as the word is incomprehensible and sounds pleasantly similar to latrine, it should be used at all possible opportunities. Moreover, latrocinium has a great and significant history. The word was first applied to the Second Council of Ephesus, a grand meeting of the fifth-century church to decide upon the exact nature of Christ and who should therefore be burnt. It was so riotous, raucous and disagreeable that the Pope declared the whole thing null and void, called it a latrocinium, and then held another council at Chalcedon, which reversed all of its decisions. As most morning meetings, like most mornings, will someday be thought better of, latrocinium has resonance.

So, everybody here? When you read the minutes of a meeting, whether it's a board-meeting, an AGM or an orgy, you will find near the top the cumbersome phrase 'apologies for absence', or in some particularly verbose cases 'apologies for non-attendance'. This can be done away with. You see, there is a single (and singularly suitable) word for that: *essoinment*.

Essoinment is the act of *essoining*, and essoining is (OED):

> To offer an excuse for the non-appearance of (a person) in court; to excuse for absence.

So all that the minutes of the meeting really need is 'Essoinments' followed by a list of names. Once the essoinments are given, the *consulting* (or being stupid together) can begin.

Eutychus in the boardroom

At any given meeting somebody is bound to go on too long, and it's usually the first speaker. It doesn't really matter if the speaker is St Paul himself, as is clear from the Book of Acts, Chapter 20:

> And upon the first day of the week, when the disciples came together to break bread, Paul preached unto them, ready to depart on the morrow; and continued his speech until midnight. And there were many lights in the upper chamber, where they were gathered together. And there sat in a window a certain young man named Eutychus, being fallen into a deep sleep: and as Paul was long preaching, he sunk down with sleep, and fell down from the third loft, and was taken up dead.

This is a story to remember if anybody ever tells you about the enthusiasm and ecstasy of the early Christians. Indeed, if there were any justice in this world or the next, Eutychus would by now be the patron saint of people who doze off during sermons.

There are all sorts of precise and technical words for exactly how somebody might bore you. For example, Henry Cockeram's *English Dictionarie* of 1623 has the word *obganiate*, which he defines as 'to trouble one with often repeating of one thing', and which comes from the Latin for 'growl'. So once the same point has been made for the umpteenth time in the umpteenth different way, you can nod and murmur 'Obganiation' as though it weren't rude.

If the obganiation comes down to the repetition of a particular word – like 'teamwork', 'delivery', or 'chryselephantine' – it becomes *battology*. Battology is named after an ancient

Greek king called Battus, who founded the city of Cyrene but is remembered in the English language only for the fact that he had a stammer. A word can be battologised so often that it relinquishes all meaning or significance and becomes a pure series of sounds that flutter around the meeting table. This is called *semantic satiation*, or 'lapse of meaning'.

But it is not merely repetition that annoys: there's some talk that is pointless in the first place. One can, for example, speculate with neither fruit nor point about how a client might react to something that will never happen, or where the company will be in twenty years' time. Such pointless speculation is technically known as *mataeology*, and such speculators as *mataeologians*.[1] And though this term of abuse is usually applied to theologians, it is as rife in the corporation as the cathedral.

Listening

In all this, the important thing is to look as though you're listening. If you are actually listening, that's even better, but let us start with simple goals. Evelyn Waugh, in his later years, used to have an ear trumpet. It probably wasn't even necessary, but he would hold it conspicuously to his shell-like during conversations, and, when he was bored, would just as conspicuously put it back in his pocket, sometimes while you were in midsentence. This is a Bad Tactic, unless you own the company.

---

[1] *Mataeology* comes from the Greek *mataios*, meaning pointless, and *logia*, meaning words. This same root also gave the English language *mataeotechny*, which means 'an unprofitable or pointless science, skill or activity'.

Much better is the method adopted by the actor Peter Lorre when he had fled the Nazis and managed to get a meeting with Alfred Hitchcock in London. Lorre knew no English, but as Hitchcock was remarkably enamoured of the sound of his own voice this was not a problem. When Lorre had to speak, he said 'Yes'. For the rest of the time:

> I had heard that [Hitchcock] loved to tell stories and so I watched him like a hawk and when I was of the opinion he had just told the punch line of a story I broke out in such laughter that I almost fell off my chair.

If you take this method and replace laughing with nodding, you have achieved all you really need to do in the morning meeting: you have become *nod-crafty*.

Nod-crafty is defined in the OED as 'Given to nodding the head with an air of great wisdom'. And once you notice nod-crafties, they're everywhere. Those who are paid to interview people on television are notoriously nod-crafty. Indeed, as many interviews are conducted with only one camera, which is pointed at the interviewee, they then have to set everything up again for a second series of shots that show nothing but the interviewer nodding. In the trade, these are called *noddies*. W.H. Auden pointed out in 1969 that a lot of doctors are nod-crafty, that's despite the fact that the OED doesn't record any uses after 1608. But the best place to observe the nod-crafty is in an art gallery. Here the nod-craftiest will approach a picture, pause, tilt up their aesthete chins for a few seconds of appreciation and then finally, with a small smile, nod. The pictures rarely nod back.

In an office meeting, being nod-crafty can be combined with *pectination*. This is when the fingers are interlaced like two combs (the Latin for comb was *pectin*). Well-pectinated fingers and a head like a rocking horse should be enough to get you through the meeting unscathed, especially if you are also wise enough to keep your mouth shut and play at *mumbudget*, a lovely old phrase for keeping quiet.

I should warn you that Sir Thomas Browne observed in his *Pseudodoxia Epidemica* (1646) that:

> To set cross leg'd, or with our fingers pectinated or shut together is accounted bad, and friends will perswade us from it.

It's at times like this that you know who your real friends are.

Argument

There are times, though, when good people have to take a stand, even at the morning meeting. Sometimes you can no longer sit there in silent *longanimity*, but must stand up and speak out for what you believe in, such as comfier chairs and a new printer. At such times you should remember Cicero before the Senate, Socrates before the Athenians, Jesus before Pilate, and that they all ended up dead. So it's probably better to follow the example of Lord Copper's underling in Evelyn Waugh's *Scoop*:

> When Lord Copper was right he said 'Definitely, Lord Copper'; when he was wrong, 'Up to a point.'

You must not simply *ding* people, ding being an eighteenth-century term for telling a chap what he really doesn't want to hear. If you tell your opponent that they're an idiot and that you'd no more take their advice on innovative teamwork than you would ask a rabbi whether to go for streaky or back, it may cause a scene. Far better to start off with the words: 'Permit me to *discept*.' And then, before anybody has a chance to grab a dictionary and discover that *discepting* means 'disagreeing utterly', you can continue with: 'I see what you're saying and it's *ultracrepidarian*.' Be careful here to put the stress on *ultra*, as words with *ultra* always sound cool.

Ultracrepidarianism is 'giving opinions on subjects that you know nothing about', and is thus a terribly useful word. Ultracrepidarian was introduced into English by the essayist William Hazlitt, but it goes back to a story about the great ancient Greek painter Apelles.

The story goes that Apelles used to leave his new paintings out on public display and then hide behind a pillar to hear people's reactions. One day he overheard a cobbler pointing out that Apelles had painted a shoe all wrong. So he took the painting away, corrected the shoe and put it out on display again the next day.

The cobbler came back, saw that Apelles had taken his advice and was so proud and puffed up with conceit that he started talking loudly about what was wrong with the leg; at which point Apelles jumped out from his hiding place and shouted: '*Ne sutor ultra crepidam*',[2] which approximately translates as 'the

---

[2] Apelles was Greek, but the only version of the story we have is in Latin.

cobbler should go no further than the shoe'. Thus *ultracrepidar-ian* literally means 'beyond-the-shoe'.

Providing that nobody else at the table knows that little story, you can use *ultracrepidarian* with impish impunity.

Though this may not provide a *sockdolager*, or winning point in an argument, it will nonetheless give you a certain gravitas and mystery that will unsettle any dictionaryless meeting. Nor should your attack end here; it should be pressed home with all the ferocity of a Vandal sacking Rome. In fact, this may be the moment to get all Cab Calloway on your colleagues' sorry bottoms.

Yes, No, Who cares?

Cabell Calloway was one of the great big-band leaders of the 1930s and 40s. He succeeded Duke Ellington at the Cotton Club, made 'Minnie the Moocher' a hit, travelled around America in a private train in which he kept his green Lincoln car, and, when not drinking and womanising his way around New York, he wrote a dictionary.

Cab Calloway's Hepsters Dictionary: Language of Jive went through six editions between 1938 and 1944, and even includes a test section and translation essays. The idea was that the lonely American, exiled in the Mid-West, Deep South or Nameless North, could prepare himself for the lingo of the Big Apple. It can also be used in the office of the present day to startling effect.

A little preparation is required. Physically, you can only speak in hepster jive if you are sitting in the correct posture:

slouched in your chair, eyelids half-down, legs stretched languidly under the table. If you have a toothpick, that's good. If you have a canary yellow suit and a tommy gun, that's better (although here you should consult the HR department about dress codes and office conduct). Now, suppose you wish to tell the speaker that you thoroughly concur and that you wish to progress their proposals proactively. Click your fingers, show some teeth and say, in the deepest voice you can: 'I dig your lick, baby, I dig your lick.'

A *lick* here is, of course, an ostinato phrase played upon the brass or the piano forte, transferred metaphorically to the office, and *dig* means … well, digging means liking for reasons that nobody is really sure of. In fact, you can go one further than digging and simply exclaim: 'That's shovel city, man!'; although this phrase should not be used without careworn consideration, particularly of gender discrimination policies.

You can even be lukewarm and still keep things jive-assed. For example, if somebody is droning on and on about stuff that everybody at the meeting already knows, lean forward intently, stare threateningly into their face and say, 'We're all breathin' natural gas', thus implying by analogy that the information they thought they were revealing for the first time is already as common as air.

Downright disagreement can be properly imparted with the simple words, 'I don't go for that magoo', and that should put an end to the subject.

So that's 'Yes', 'No' and 'Who cares?', which is all you really need in life, and usually more than you need in the office where two of those will do. You can, if you like, take this principle further. Why stop at 1930s New York when you can go back to

Victorian London and act like a sweet-faced orphan or under-nourished Dickensian crossing sweeper? Of course, the costume is more demanding, but if your meeting room does have a chimney then you can burst out of it at the vital moment and register agreement by shouting 'That's screamin', mister!' And 'I'm breathin' natural gas' has its equivalent in the words 'I've seen the elephant, chum', a reference to the fact that the travelling circuses of Victorian England had made elephants commonplace to all but the most bumpkinish of rustics. 'No' can be rendered by the enigmatic expression 'Saw your timber'.

Mugwumpery

Whatever age or idiom you elect to use, the truth remains that if an argument breaks out everybody will start piling in. It's what schoolboys at Winchester College would have called a *Mons* (whereby everybody jumps on top of one boy for reasons that remain suspicious). You are no longer a *conventicle* of thoughtful professionals, you are *Dover Court*: all speakers and no listeners.[3] And it is time for a *mugwump* to step in.

A mugwump is a derogatory word for somebody in charge who affects to be above petty squabbles and factions. So when your boss tries to make peace at the meeting table like an impartial angel, he is being a mugwump.

---

[3] The church at Dover Court in Essex once contained a speaking crucifix, which may be the origin of this expression. Apparently, the crucifix insisted that the church doors were never shut, and it was therefore filled with chattering pilgrims, which may also be the origin. Unfortunately, the cross was burnt to ashes by Protestants in 1532, so we can no longer ask its opinion.

Mugwump is therefore an eminently useful word. It has a preposterous sound: the *ug* and the *ump* get across the idea of plodding stupidity, and context can give it meaning.

The origin of the word is rather extraordinary and involves the first American Bible.

There was a seventeenth-century chap called John Eliot who was a Protestant, a Puritan and a colonist in America. He wanted to convert the local natives – the Wampanoag – to Christianity and to do so he needed a Bible in their language. He learnt Massachusett, the language of the Wampanoags, and then had to invent a writing system to get it down on paper. The result was Eliot's Massachusett Bible of 1663: the first Bible ever printed in America.

Eliot had the perennial translator's problem of finding words for concepts that don't exist in a language. The Wampanoags had no centurions, no captains, no generals, and so what was he to do when such fellows cropped up in the Bible? He decided to translate all of them using the Wampanoag word for war leader: *mugquomp*.

Mugwump then disappeared for 150 years. There is neither citation nor quotation until the early nineteenth century when it reappears as a comical and derisive term for a boss.[4]

---

[4] So long is the silence that some say John Eliot's *mugquomp* has nothing to do with the nineteenth-century *mugwump*. The OED avers that there is no reason to connect the two. I might believe the OED, were it not that the first modern *mugwump* it cites is from Vermont in 1828. Vermont is only just to the north of the Wampanoag homeland. This alone would test coincidence to the limit. The second citation is from Rhode Island in 1832 and Rhode Island is slap bang in the middle of Wampanoag territory. Had *mugwump* reappeared in California or Dorset, I might credit it as an independent coinage. But geography being what

Mugwumpery can be dealt with in two ways. You can return to hepcat jive-talking and shout 'Get off the fence, Hortense!' This is an example of the mid-century American craze for throwing in a rhyming word at the end of a sentence, e.g. 'See you later, alligator', or 'What's on the agenda, Brenda?' or 'The figures from the third quarter are disappointing but we're confident that we have the sales team in place to make progress in this exciting sector, Hector'.

The other way to deal with mugwumpery is to accept it and switch to *log-rolling*, which is an American term derived from the phrase 'You roll my log, and I'll roll yours'. Log-rolling can therefore refer to the mutual and excruciatingly boring exchange of praise and plaudits, as everybody agrees that everybody else is just super. There's even a specialist term, *literary log-rolling*, that refers to authors writing complimentary reviews of each other's dreary tomes. There should be an example on the back.

Discretion

And now, once the *contekors* have stopped quarrelling, the dust has settled and everybody has resolved on a course of *aboulia* (indecisiveness) and *periergy* (needless caution), the morning meeting can finally be wrapped up. Anything further would be *supervacaneous*. Most importantly, we should leave now before anybody mentions the *tacenda*. Tacenda are those things that must never be mentioned, like the fact that the company is effectively bankrupt or overstaffed or in breach of child labour

---

it is, I am as certain as certain can be that *mugwump* is *mugquomp*, and that the first American Bible produced a fine American insult.

laws, or all three. In fact, the tacenda is the absolute opposite of the agenda: those *nefandous* words that the tongue of man should never utter in front of his colleagues, but must instead be dedicated in reverent hush to Harpocrates, the ancient and terrible god of silence.

So take your harpocratic oath, gather up your things and dash out of the meeting room. You may even have time for a quick *earnder*, which is an old Yorkshire term for a morning drinking session.

Chapter 6

11 a.m. – Taking a Break

Coffee – gossip – incredulity – cigarette

❦

Since mankind first mastered the concept of the time, eleven o'clock has been the sacred hour of the mid-morning break. It is the holy hour of tea or coffee, and possibly a biscuit. At the eleventh chime of the clock, spring into inaction.

Even bears hold this *undecimarian* hour to be a time of eating and idleness, as is witnessed in the first book of *Winnie the Pooh*, Chapter 2:

> Pooh always liked a little something at eleven o'clock in the morning, and he was very glad to see Rabbit getting out the plates and mugs; and when Rabbit said, 'Honey or condensed milk with your bread?' he was so excited that he said, 'Both,' and then, so as not to seem greedy, he added, 'But don't bother about the bread, please.'

There are all sorts of words for this snack: *elevenses* (Kentish dialect), *dornton* (northern), *eleven hours* (Scottish), *eleven o'clock* (American) and *elevener* (Suffolk). An elevener is best, as it includes the possibility of a drink or tipple, whereas all the rest are teetotalitarian.

Of course, you mustn't be lazy. It is important to work energetically at your coffee- or tea-making.[1] You may bustle around with the mugs and spoons while the kettle *thrumbles* (makes that rumbling noise just before it boils). And that thrumbling will act as a summons to all the office gossips.

The word for a person who always wants to know the latest gossip and scandal is a *quidnunc*, which is Latin for 'what now?' The practice of being a quidnunc is called either *quidnuncism* or, slightly more delightfully, *quidnuncery*. There's even an alternative term, *numquid*, which means exactly the same thing: 'now what' instead of 'what now'. So as the tea brews, the water cools or the coffee percolates, it is time to drop your voices and *quother*, or speak in low tones of firings, hirings, of bonks and rumours of bonks.

Even if you don't want to know 'what now', you will probably be told anyway. The following is from a dictionary of late eighteenth-century slang, but it rings terribly true today:

> FIRING A GUN, Introducing a story by head and shoulders.
> A man wanting to tell a particular story, said to the company,
> Hark! did you not hear a gun? – but now we are talking of a
> gun, I will tell you the story of one.

Now they all come out: the rumours, *furphies* and strange tidings – the pure joy of being a *rawgabbit* and a *spermologer*. A rawgabbit, just in case you were wondering, is somebody who speaks in strictest confidence about a subject of which they

---

[1] In the eighteenth century they used to mix tea and coffee together and call it *twist*. In the interests of scholarship I tried this myself and do not recommend that anybody else does.

know nothing. A rawgabbit is the person who pulls you aside and reveals in a careful whisper that the head of Compliance is having an affair with the new recruit in IT, which you know to be utterly untrue because the head of Compliance is having an affair with you, and the new recruit in IT hasn't started yet. Nonetheless, as a careful spermologer you mustn't reveal that you know too much. Being a spermologer isn't nearly as mucky as it sounds. Though it does come from the Greek for seed-gathering, spermologer's use in English is a metaphorical one for a gatherer of gossip and a seeker after scurrilous rumours.

You may begin to feel that you are in what Second World War soldiers called a *bind*.

> **Bind**. This must be the most used of all Air Force slang expressions. It may describe a person who bores with out-of-date news or who is always in the know.

Hence:

> **Binding rigid.** The act of continually retailing stale information.

Disbelief

Actually, though we are beside the kettle, most of the best rumours are started in the lavatory. The technical term for a story started in the lavatories is *latrinogram*, from *gram* being writing in Greek and *latrine* being, well, a latrine. Latrinogram is first recorded in 1944 as a British military term and was probably where guesses as to the date of D-Day were exchanged.

So popular were wartime lavatories as a source of gossip that there's a similar and slightly earlier version of latrinogram: *Elsan gen*, which is defined in a 1943 dictionary of services slang thus:

> **Elsan gen**: News which cannot be relied upon. [Literally, 'news invented in the gentlemen's toilet', Elsan being the trade name of the excellent chemical lavatories with which bombers are equipped.]

I'm not sure exactly how you would fit two people into the lavatories of an RAF bomber, or why indeed you would wish to do so. The rumble and thrumble of the engines might also make it hard to exchange the juiciest furphies in an appropriate quother. It therefore looks to me as though *Elsan gen* was a circumlocutory manner of saying that the information (or gen) was equivalent in quality to the stuff physically produced in such a cubby hole, and therefore fit only to be flushed out over Axis territory.

Soldiers of the Second World War seem to have spent as much time gossiping as fighting, if their slang is anything to go by. Aside from Elsan gen, they had *duff gen* (bad), *pukka gen* (good) and the *gen king* (the chap who knew all of the gossip before it had even happened).

All of the best rumours are false. The more that you yearn to believe a good yarn, the more likely it is that that yarn is mere *flim-flam*, *flumadiddle*, *fribble-frabble*, *effutiation*, *flitter-tripe*, *rhubarb*, *spinach*, *toffee*, *waffle*, *balductum* and *bollocks*.

This leaves the question of how you should respond to the Elsan gen. The politest method would be to tell your interlocutor that they are a *controver*, an obsolete word for an 'inventor of false gossip'. Though it's recorded in a dictionary of 1721 the word, for some reason, never caught on or even made it into any subsequent dictionaries. This strange vanishing means that you can call somebody a controver to your heart's content and they'll never know what you mean. Thus the cogs of office society can remain oily.

Alternatively, you can exclaim, as the Victorians would have done, that a story is 'all my eye and Betty Martin'. The origins of this phrase are rather peculiar. The story goes that a British sailor happened to wander into a church in some foreign and Roman Catholic country. There he heard a prayer which of course sounded like nonsense to him because it was in Latin. So far as the sailor could tell, they were saying something along the lines of 'All my eye and Betty Martin'. The original prayer was probably *Ora pro mihi, beate Martine* or 'Pray for me, blessed Martin', Saint Martin of Tours being the patron saint of innkeepers and reformed drunkards. Alternatively, it could have been *Mihi beata mater* or 'For me blessed Mother', making Betty Martin the Virgin Mary. So if you want to be sure not to blaspheme, you could just call your story-teller a *blatherskite* or *clanjanderer*. Or you could take a lesson from this singular dictionary entry:

DICK That happened in the reign of queen Dick, i.e. never: said of any absurd old story. I am as queer as Dick's hatband; that is, out of spirits, or don't know what ails me.[2]

This is my personal favourite, as it usually takes the other party a couple of seconds to figure it out.

---

[2] The second half of that entry is irrelevant, but much too much fun to leave out.

Honesty is as under-represented in the dictionary as in life. It makes occasional appearances, such as:

> BUFFING IT HOME is swearing point-blank to anything, about the same as bluffing it, making a bold stand on no backing.

But that's taken from an 1881 dictionary of New York criminal slang, so it doesn't fill you with confidence. The best you can do is a *corsned*, which was a part of ancient English law:

> **Corsned**, Ordeal bread, a Piece of Bread consecrated by the Priest for that Use, eaten by the Saxons when they would clear themselves of a Crime they were charged with, wishing it might be their Poison, or last Morsel, if they were guilty.

As we are having elevenses, you may simply reach for the nearest chocolate biscuit.

Finally, there is the gossip that has neither the virtue of truth nor the fun of falsehood, and is merely old. A standard riposte to hearing old news is to say 'Queen Anne is dead'. The phrase is first recorded in 1798 (Queen Anne having died in 1714), but it's still used in British journalistic circles. It's a slightly out of date expression for being out of date, but it does have the virtue of finality. And having informed your colleagues of the monarch's demise, you may sneak off for a cigarette.

Cigarettes

James VI of Scotland and I of England was a *misocapnist*, i.e. he didn't like smokers or smoking one little bit. In 1604 he wrote a pamphlet about how much he didn't like smokers called *A Counter-Blaste to Tobacco*. A few years later the Bishop of Winchester translated *Counter-Blaste* into Latin. Why anybody would have bothered translating an anti-smoking tract into Latin is beyond me, but that didn't stop the Bishop of Winchester. He called the translation the *Misocapnus*, which is Latin for 'against smoke', and the word blew gently into the English language as *misocapnist* (the noun) and *misocapnic* (the adjective).

The primary reason that James I didn't like tobacco was that it was a habit newly imported from the American Indians, whom he thought simply horrible. He asks his subjects:

> ... shall we, I say, without blushing, abase our selves so farre, as to imitate these beastly Indians, slaves to the Spaniards, refuse to the world, and as yet aliens from the holy Covenant of God? Why doe we not as well imitate them in walking naked as they doe? in preferring glasses, feathers, and such toyes, to golde and precious stones, as they do? yea why do we not denie God and adore the Devill, as they doe?

Does that put you off your ciggy? No? Then off we go to our fag break (or *smoko* as the Australians call it). But first, it would be only polite for you to ask some of your co-workers if they wish to come along for a puff. The best way to word such an

invitation can be found in a dictionary of highwayman's slang
from 1699:

Will ye raise a Cloud, shall we Smoke a Pipe?

It's best to ask this in a raspy, piratish voice and, if possible, to
carry a blunderbuss. But you can't smoke here. The misocapnic
ghost of James I still haunts us all with smokeless restrictions
and rules, and so you will probably not be able to raise a cloud
at your own desk and must instead retreat to a designated smoking area, an indignity that was never suffered by highwaymen.

'Designated smoking area' is an unnecessarily wordy and
official name for a *fumatorium* or even better, a *coughery*, which
is a place where people go to cough. Sir Thomas Urquhart wrote
that before a service, priests:

> … dunged in the dungeries, pissed in the pisseries, spit in the
> spiteries, coughed in the cougheries and doted in the doteries,
> that to the Divine Service they might not bring any Thing that
> was unclean or foul.

Even though Urquhart wasn't being thoroughly serious about
that, coughery is still as good a name as any for the little yard by the
office's back door where a forlorn but persistent *tabagie* still holds
out like the last remnants of a dying Amazonian tribe. A tabagie,
by the way, is the technical term for a group of smokers, although
the collective noun (as in a *pride of lions* or a *murder of crows*) is
a *parliament of smokers*. Both words emerged in the nineteenth
century, the high-point of fumious vocabulary. For the Victorian,
a smoker was not merely a smoker, he was a *tobacconalian* or a

nicotinian. So if you don't feel like using 'coughery' and 'raising a cloud' you could always escape from the misocapnists by taking 'a voyage to the Land of the Nicotinians'.

The Land of the Nicotinians would be a fabulous place: shrouded in impenetrable clouds and dotted with naturally occurring humidors. There the obedient Nicotinians would do homage before their goddess Nicotia, and no, I didn't just make her up. Nicotia too is an invention of Victorian poetry. The American poet James Russell Lowell even wrote in the 1860s about her divine lineage. She was, according to him, the daughter of Bacchus, god of revelry, and her mother was the daughter of Morpheus, god of dreams.

> Now the kind nymph to Bacchus born
> By Morpheus' daughter, she that seems
> Gifted upon her natal morn
> By him with fire, by her with dreams,
> Nicotia, dearer to the Muse
> Than all the grape's bewildering juice,
> We worship, unforbid of thee ...

But the goddess can't even protect her poor worshippers who, persecuted by the malevolent misocapnists, are forced to raise their clouds in distant pavement cougheries in the wind and the rain.

And why? Because smoking is considered unhealthy (and Red Indian). But it was not always thus! Once upon a time there was no great divide between the sporty and the smoky, because smoking *was* a sport. There was such a thing as a *smoking match*. It is recorded in Joseph Strutt's *Sports and Pastimes of the People of England* (1801) in an entry between 'Grinning Matches' and 'Hot Hasty-Pudding Eaters'.

> **Smoking matches** are usually made for tobacco-boxes, or some other trifling prizes, and may be performed two ways: the first is a trial among the candidates who shall smoke a pipe full of tobacco in the shortest time: the second is precisely the reverse; for he of them who can keep the tobacco alight within his pipe, and retain it there the longest, receives the reward.

Smoking matches were filled with twists and turns and yellow-nail-biting excitement. Consider this match report from 1723, when men were men and smoking was a competitive sport:

> Oxford, a scaffold being built up for it just at Finmore's, an ale-house. The conditions were, that anyone (man or woman) that could smoak out three ounces of tobacco first, without drinking or going off the stage, should have twelve shillings. Many tryed, and 'twas thought that a journeyman taylour, of St Peters in the East, would have been victor, he smoaking faster than, and being many pipes before, the rest; but at last he was so sick, that 'twas thought he would have dyed; and an old man, that had been a souldier, and smoaked gently, came off conquerour, smoaking the three ounces quite out, and he told one, (from whom I had it,) that, after it, he smoaked four or five pipes the same evening.

In the seventeenth century smokers were even given the ridiculously romantic title of *fume gallants*, conjuring an image of white knights with yellow teeth. There used to be none of this nonsense about smoking being bad for you. In fact it was once generally recognised (but since covered up by misocapnist spoilsports) that smoking cures you (a fact that has always been known to salmon). Hence a medical dictionary of 1859 contains this fascinating entry:

> INSUFFLATION (*in*, in; *sufflo*, to blow). The act of blowing a
> gas or vapour into a cavity of the body, as when tobacco smoke
> is injected into the rectum, or air blown into the lungs, &c.

I don't know how useful that word will be to you; but if the necessity ever arises, you will at least know what to call it.

Anyhow, having arrived in the tabagie, you must now obtain a cigarette (the cost these days being such that nobody at all buys their own). The correct 1950s way to ask for a smoke is 'Butt me', which works very well unless you're talking to a ram. If you are among particularly generous company, somebody may even offer you a cancer stick without being asked, in which case they should, if they wish to be equally 1950s, accompany their generosity with the kind words, 'Have a firework'.

Of course, the problem with accepting cigarettes from others is that they may smoke a different kind of coffin nail to you. For example, you may be offered a *straight*, or manufactured ciga-rette, when what you were really after was a *quirly* which you roll yourself. And even if you and your patron are in agreement that smoking should be an arts and crafty type of affair, their favourite tobacco may be to you little more than *mundungus*, which is 'bad, or rank tobacco', also called *old rope*.

Now that you have something tobaccical, look around for a *salamander*, or 'red hot iron used for lighting tobacco'. If none has been provided, you may settle for an entry in

Dr Johnson's dictionary:

> **Sponk**. A word in Edinburgh which denotes a match, or any
> thing dipt in sulphur that takes fire: as, *any sponks will ye buy?*

Once you have a sponk you may *cock your organ* (light your
pipe) and begin to *funk*. Funk was the standard term for smoking from the late seventeenth century through to the early nineteenth, when it suddenly started to mean a panic attack, and
then in the twentieth century it became a kind of music. Funk
was also, by association, a term for tobacco smoke, which means
that you are currently smelling rather *funky*.

Ashcan used to be a slang term for wasted time. So unfortunately you must funk as fast as you can and then remember the
poor of the parish. This from a dictionary of Victorian slang:

> HARD-UPS, cigar-end finders, who collect the refuse pieces
> of smoked cigars from the gutter, and having dried them, sell
> them as tobacco to the very poor.

So don't whatever you do stamp out your stub. Remember the
hard-ups, and remember those devilish Red Indians that James
I hated. But why rely on his misocapnist claptrap? Instead we
can use an actual account of tobacco in the New World: the very
first written record of the human smoking. It's from Gonzalo
Fernandez de Oviedo, who visited Hispaniola in 1535 and
recorded how the native chieftain would smoke until he passed
out and then 'his wives, who are many, pick him up, and carry
him to his hammock'.

But not for you! Back to your desk, and pretend to work.

Chapter 7

Noon – Looking as Though You're Working

Effortlessness – sales and marketing – emails –
approaching bankruptcy – asking for a raise

⌒⌒⌒

Sprezzatura, or the nonchalance of the perfect office worker

It is probably time to do some work, or at least appear to. Work, like justice, must not only be done, it must be seen to be done. Appearances are everything, reality an inconvenience.

In the Renaissance, there was an exquisite idea named *sprezzatura*, the nonchalance of the perfect courtier. It was the newest and most fashionable thing once. You see, all through the medieval period, knights had known what they had to do: they had to be knights in armour. They had to be chivalrous to ladies of course, but they also had to be warlike and violent and bloodthirsty. When the Renaissance came along the bar was raised somewhat. Skill at arms was still valued, but suddenly a man was expected to stop being medieval and be Renaissance, which meant learning to do all sorts of things like read, write, paint, play a few instruments, speak Latin, appreciate sculpture and whatnot.

These new requirements were handily laid out in a sort of textbook by Baldassare Castiglione. Castiglione was the very model of a modern courtier and peregrinated around Italy being a friend of Raphael and the Medicis. He was an ambassador, a classicist, a soldier and a sonneteer. And he wrote a book about how you too could be like him. It was called *The Book of the Courtier*, was translated into every language anyone could think of, and for centuries afterwards was the European definition of the Perfect Man. However, there was one word in it that could never quite be translated properly: *sprezzatura*.

Sprezzatura sort of means nonchalance, but more precisely it means the appearance of nonchalance – the effort made to disguise the fact that you're making an effort. So you should be a brilliant musician, for example, but nobody should ever see or hear you practise. Thus you take your flute or lute or whatever and disappear well out of earshot and work at your musicianship in secret. Then when somebody says, 'Hey, Baldassare, do you play the lute at all?', you can reply, 'The lute? Hmm. I've never tried but pass it here … Oh, like this?' – and then knock off a little virtuoso performance while looking bored. Everybody gasps in astonishment at your effortless ability, and you appear much better than you would have done had the whole court heard you plink plonk plunking for months on end.

This Great Untranslatable, graceful nonchalance hiding discreet diligence, simply had to be imported into the other European languages including English, where the OED defines it as 'studied carelessness'.

But the Renaissance is dead and done, and with it sprezzatura has wandered nonchalantly from the language. It has been replaced, though, by that most horrible of ideas: *presenteeism*, the belief that you should be the first in and the last to leave and do nothing in between because it's not work but the appearance of work that is rewarded.

But imagine, just imagine, if sprezzatura were brought back to the modern office. Gone would be those dreary press releases saying 'Flumshoe Incorporated are really excited about this new acquisition! John Splunkington, Head of Mergers, said: "I want to thank everybody on the team who have put in the long hours over the last year to make this deal happen."' Instead, you would have: 'Flumshoe Incorporated is filled with languorous indifference at this new acquisition. John Splunkington, who lolls gracefully around the mergers department, murmured: "It was nothing. A trifle really", and continued to play his lute.'

Earning a living

But sprezzatura is gone, and it is time to actually sit down at your desk and *quomodocunquize*. Quomodocunquizing is 'making money in any way that you can', and was used in this glorious phrase by Sir Thomas Urquhart in 1652: 'Those quomodocunquizing clusterfists and rapacious varlets.'

A *clusterfist* is, as you might imagine, somebody who keeps a tight grip on his cash. Quomodocunquizing can be used of governments, football clubs, famous people who advertise things, and of course yourself. For we are quomodocunquizing animals. It is the chief symptom of *plutomania*, which is 'the frenzied pursuit of money'.

In case you were wondering, the planet Pluto is named after the god of the underworld. As gold and silver and diamonds are always found underground, the ancients decided that Pluto was also the god of money, hence plutomania, *plutocracy* (government by the rich), *plutography* (written descriptions of the lives of the rich) and *plutolatry* (worship of wealth).

The best course for the aspiring plutomaniac is to become a *plutogogue*, which can mean either somebody who speaks only to the rich or somebody who speaks only for them. The former is commonly known as sales, and the latter advertising, but plutogogue is a much more impressive word to put on your business card or CV.

If you would prefer, though, to have a more rough-and-ready feel to your job description in sales, you could always describe yourself as a *barker*, which was the Victorian term for somebody who stood outside a shop shouting its virtues into the smoggy air. Unfortunately, Victorian slang dictionaries also contain this entry:

> CHUFF IT, *i.e.*, be off, or take it away, in answer to a street seller who is importuning you to purchase.

A useful phrase for dealing with cold callers.

Email

These days, the telephone is used less and less and email more and more. It's enough to bring back the noble business of *screeving*. A screever is a professional writer of begging letters.

These letters would not be sent, rather they would be given to somebody else who would use them as a sort of certificate of authenticity as they told their hard luck story. Luckily for historians of strange trades, a typical Victorian screever's price list survives:

Friendly letter 6d
Long ditto 9d
Petition 1s
Ditto with signatures 1s 6d
Ditto with forged names 2s 6d
Ditto 'very heavy' (dangerous) 3s
Manuscript for a broken-down author 10s
Part of a play for ditto 7s 6d

It is somehow comforting to know that there were broken-down authors even then.

There's something rather nasty about the sound of the word *screever* that makes it less than wholesome. It's a mixture of *scream* and *grieve* and would not look good on the résumé. If you want a more high-flying term for a writer of begging letters, the Victorians also called them *high fliers*.

Once you have screeved and flown high, the matter is up to the *answer jobber*, who is, as you may have guessed, a professional writer of answers. This is the way most of us spend at least the first half hour of our day at the desk, picking through the emails that have accumulated like dew in the night.

It's a shame that there are not, as yet, any particularly beautiful names for kinds of email. In the days of pen and paper, a little letter could be called a *notekin* or a *breviate* or a *letterling*, but a short email is a short email and nobody seems to be doing much about it. Some of the terms for letters can be saved, though. For example, an *omnibus letter* – one intended for several recipients – could easily become an 'omnibus email' and replace the tedious 'group email'. In fact, here is a list of the possibilities, in which I have simply replaced 'letter' with 'email' and provided the old definition.

Bread and butter email – one saying thank you.

Cheddar email – one to which several people have contributed, just as several dairies contribute to a single cheddar cheese.

Email of comfort – one that assures a creditor that a debt will be paid, without being legally binding.

Journal email – one that talks about what you've been up to lately.

Email of placards – one that grants permission.

Email of marque – one that allows you to behave like a pirate. These should be sent sparingly. (Letters of marque would be sent out to ships' captains when war was declared, allowing them to plunder the merchant ships of the enemy nation.)

Laureate email – one announcing victory.

Email of Uriah – 'A treacherous email, implying friendship, but in reality a death warrant', thus (almost) *Brewer's Dictionary of Phrase and Fable*. I send a lot of these. The name refers to the Second Book of Samuel: 'And it came to pass in the morning, that David wrote a letter to Joab, and sent it by the hand of

Uriah. And he wrote in the letter, saying, Set ye Uriah in the forefront of the hottest battle, and retire ye from him, that he may be smitten, and die.'

Once the emails are finished with, there are all sorts of jobs for a busy *jobler* to do (a jobler is somebody who does small jobs). You could rearrange the stuff on your desk, update your status on the interweb, or you could work hard as a *nephelolater* (one who admires passing clouds). Whatever you do, though, don't look at the accounts unless you have *audit ale*.

Audit ale was a specially strong and tasty kind of ale to be drunk only on the day of an audit. You can't buy it any more. You couldn't even buy it back in 1823 when Byron wrote 'The Age of Bronze', lamenting the fallen state of modern Britain and asking:

> Where is it now, the goodly audit ale,
> The purse-proud tenant never known to fail?

And you can't do an audit without an audit ale, because you should never look at your finances without a good strong drink in your hand. Bankruptcy looks so much better through the bottom of a bottle. If ale-sodden insolvency does beckon, all that you can do is grab what you can while you can. A pleasant little word for this is *deaconing*. A dictionary of Americanisms from 1889 has this helpful definition:

> To deacon land, to filch land by gradually extending one's fences or boundary lines into the highway or other common property.

So move that pile of papers just a little onto your podmate's desk, and dream of slow victories and distant laureate emails.

Deaconing can also mean 'putting the most attractive goods on the top of a pile' or 'watering down liquor' or 'killing a calf the second it is born'. Why it should mean this nobody knows, but all the phrases are American and nineteenth-century, so one must imagine that nineteenth-century American deacons were all dishonest, acquisitive, calf-murdering scoundrels.

Asking for a raise

If you have been deaconing for long enough and have acquired enough territory, it may even be time to ask for a raise. This must be done with tact and discretion. Begin by approaching your boss in a *sardonian* manner. A sardonian is, according to the OED, 'one who flatters with deadly intent'. The reason for this odd and unusually precise word is not a person but a plant. The *herba sardonia* was said to cause horrible facial convulsions that resembled laughter, followed by death.

You don't need to kill your boss, of course, but a bit of calculated *glavering* and flattery will take the bitter edge off any *rogitating* you happen to do (to rogitate is to ask again and again for the same thing, in the manner of a child who wants a biscuit). You could try the other route, and just call your paymaster a miser and a *sting-bum* every time they walk past, but people don't like being called a sting-bum and it could all end up being counterproductive.

Then there's the Indian custom of *Dharna*. In east India, if somebody hasn't paid their debt to you, you go and sit on their doorstep and refuse to eat. You stay there until a) the person pays up or b) you starve to death. Dharna should not be attempted with somebody who lives in an out of the way place, or who takes long holidays. But in a workplace where there are lots of other people wandering around, sitting by the door of your boss's office growing slowly thinner and thinner is bound to produce some sort of effect.

You may not get a real raise today, but you might at least get a *brevet*, which is a military term for a rise in rank without a rise in salary. Brevets are usually accompanied with a nice wodge of *Spanish money*, which is an old term for 'fair words and compliments'. And that should be enough to keep you going till lunch. Until then, you may simply *fudgel*:

To Fudgel, to make a Shew of doing somewhat to no Purpose, to trifle.

Chapter 8

1 p.m. – Lunch

Where to eat – who pays – The Free Lunch – eating
– eating turtles – indigestion

❧❧❧

It is the *amell*, which is to say the hour between one and two o'clock when all right-thinking creatures rush joyously from their labours to their lunch. You hardly need a clock to know that this grand hour is at hand, as your own belly will chime with impatient *borborygmi*, the rumbling noises produced by an empty stomach. H.G. Wells once wrote that:

> ... few creatures seem to have found their 'perfect' food or, hav-
> ing found it, are able to keep to it: elephant hunters say they
> can tell the proximity of a herd by the borborygmic (see dic-
> tionary) noises the poor brutes emit, and Glasfurd describes
> a tiger's life as an alternation of uncomfortable hunger and
> uncomfortable repletion.

Better, as the saying goes, to live one day as an uncomfortable tiger, than a hundred years as a borborygmic elephant. The human is a *famelicose* (or constantly hungry) creature. And so to lunch!

But where? It seems a shame to visit the same sandwich shop every day, and anyway, you might be taking somebody out to lunch on expenses. Even if you are denied this fundamental right of luncheon by fate or your boss, you may simply be struck with a sudden case of *allotriophagy*, which is 'the desire, – the morbid longing, – to devour extraordinary substances commonly regarded as inedible, innutritious, or even hurtful'. It is thus a suitable term for anybody who suggests going to a kebab shop. Etymologically, though, it simply means a desire to eat other things, and it can therefore be used to break away from the old haunts rather than go to the same old *slap-bang shop*:

> **Slap-bang shop**, a petty cook's shop where there is no credit given, but what is had must be paid down with the ready slap-bang, i.e. immediately. This is a common appellation for a night cellar frequented by thieves, and sometimes for a stage coach or caravan. (1785)

If you want to go to a grander grubbery, you'll have to either find the cash, credit or, if possible, a *Sir Timothy*. Sir Timothy (sometimes known as *Sir Timothy Treat-All*) was a mythical figure recorded from the late seventeenth to the early nineteenth century who bought lunch. It was, and still can be, the title of 'One that Treats every Body and pays the Reckonings every where'.

The politer and more recondite term for such a saviour is *gastrophilanthropist*. That's from the Greek *gastro* meaning stomach (as in a gastropod that walks on its tummy) and *philanthropist* which means lover of men (but not in that way). Gastrophilanthropy is a sadly forgotten art, as people these days tend to give their money to feed the starving on the other side of the earth, rather than the peckish on this, and have thus substituted charity for kindness.

If you can find a suitably pliable Sir Timothy then you can settle down to some serious *scambling*. A scambler is defined in Dr Johnson's dictionary thus:

> **Scambler**: A bold intruder upon one's generosity or table. [Scottish]

By which he didn't of course mean that all scamblers are Scottish, only that enough of them are for the word to have become necessary in that country first. A scambler is the only sensible eater of lunch, for the exquisite cost of most restaurants destroys the palate, whereas the knowledge that you are dining on the gastrophilanthropy of a careless Sir Timothy allows you to fill your belly without evacuating your pocket.

One way to enter into a career as a scambler is to *groke*, which is to stare wistfully at somebody while they are eating in the hope that they will give you some of their food. Groking was originally applied only to dogs, who have this habit down to a wide-eyed T. But it can just as well be applied to the hopeful scambler or anybody who sidles over to your desk when you're eating a biscuit.

But back to lunch, or more precisely, to the preparations and *precibals* thereto and of. A precibal, by the way, is another way of saying preprandial, but which can be applied to any meal including breakfast, elevenses and midnight snacks. And speaking of preprandials, what are we having to drink? In the eighteenth century the idea of not having a drink with lunch was considered so bestial that it was referred to as a *horse's meal*: as dry as straw and fit only for an animal. So it is probably best to bid adieu to any hopes for afternoon productivity now.

Actually, alcohol is the founder of that elusive snark known as the Free Lunch. People have been insisting since the 1930s that the Free Lunch does not exist in the wild, and would lock it up in that chimerical menagerie where are stored the unicorn, the phoenix and the bunyip. But the Free Lunch is not mythical, though it may be extinct. It was observed in its natural habitat by Rudyard Kipling. In 1891 Kipling visited San Francisco and observed the Free Lunch hiding behind a bunch of spittoons.

> In a vast marble-paved hall, under the glare of an electric light, sat forty or fifty men, and for their use and amusement were provided spittoons of infinite capacity and generous gape. Most of the men wore frock-coats and top-hats – the things that we in India put on at a wedding-break-fast, if we possess them – but they all spat. They spat on principle. The spittoons were on the staircases, in each bedroom – yea, and in chambers even more sacred than these. They chased one into retirement, but they blossomed in chiefest splendor round the bar, and they were all used, every reeking one of them … By instinct I sought refreshment, and came upon a bar-room full of bad Salon pictures in which men with hats on the backs of their heads were wolfing food from a counter. It was the institution of the 'free lunch' I had struck. You paid for a drink and got as much as you wanted to eat. For something less than a rupee a day a man can feed himself sumptuously in San Francisco, even though he be a bankrupt. Remember this if ever you are stranded in these parts.

Perhaps the Free Lunch is perished for ever like the dodo – too delicious to live long; or perhaps like the shy coelacanth it lurks forever unchanged and unchanging in some cold ocean canyon that we do not know. The only way to test for its existence is to order a drink and see what happens. And remember: you're not drunk if you can still read the menu.

Mrs Beeton (1836–65) was the tragic goddess of the British kitchen. She had four children, wrote a book containing 900 recipes, and dropped down dead at the age of 28. In her author-itative gospel *Mrs Beeton's Book of Household Management* she recommends the following light luncheon:

> The remains of cold joints, nicely garnished, a few sweets, or a little hashed meat, poultry or game, are the usual articles placed on the table for luncheon, with bread and cheese bis-cuits, butter, &c. If a substantial meal is desired, rump-steaks or mutton chops may be served, as also veal cutlets, kidneys, or any dish of that kind.

It may be best to simply cut that paragraph out of the book and calmly hand it to your one o'clock waiter. Then the eating can begin.

Mastication

The traditional cry announcing that those at the table should start eating is 'Fall-a-bord!' At which point you, and all your trenchermates, may start to gobble, gourmandise and *guttle*. The last of these words, meaning 'eat greedily', is the solid food companion to the more liquid *guzzle*. It seems a terrible shame that one of these should have died out, especially as they make such a pretty couple. Indeed, if you want to make the twins near-identical you can *guttle* your food and *guddle* your drink. It is especially convenient for the enthusiastic *gutguddler* that both words can be pronounced with your mouth full or while swallowing.

In fact, there's something just a little bit greedy about the letter G. For a gourmand who gluttonously guttles and guddles too much will end up as a *gundy-guts*, which is a pleasantly eighteenth-century way of saying 'lard-arse'.

Of the seven deadly sins only three are enjoyable: gluttony, sloth and lust balance their lethality with fun. If somebody could only think of a way of combining the three, humanity would go to Hell quite happily. The procession would be accompanied by *tooth music*, which is the sound of jolly eating that serenades all the best lunches.

Another term for thorough chewing is *Fletcherism*. Horace Fletcher (1849–1919) wrote hugely influential books on how the whole human condition can be improved by chewing. He recommended 32 chews per mouthful, and even took the seemingly unnecessary precaution of chewing his drinks. He thus became, according to him, one of the fittest men alive, and earned the grand title of 'The Great Masticator'. Such was his fame and the power of his jaws that a movement sprang up known as Fletcherism, whose adherents were called *Fletcherites* and who didn't just chew their food, but *Fletcherized* it. Thus Henry James could write to his brother: 'It is impossible, save in a long talk, to make you understand how the blessed fletcherism – so extra blessed – lulled me, charmed me, beguiled me.'

He even once commented that Fletcher had so improved his bowel movements that he 'saved my life, and what is more, he improved my disposition. By rights he should receive all my future royalties.' P.G. Wodehouse, on the other hand, merely used the word *fletcherize* in a description of a mongrel attacking a terrier.

It should perhaps be noted here that Gladstone was also a proponent of chewing every gobbet 32 times, and a sly onlooker at dinner once reckoned that he averaged 70 mastications per mouthful. However, if you look up Gladstone in the dictionary, you will find that he only gave his name to a bag and to cheap French wine, on which he reduced the importation taxes. So it may now be time to order another bottle.

But perhaps you have no appetite. Rather than being an *esquire trenchant*, you merely *pingle* your food, which is a sure prognosticator of melancholy. To pingle is to push food around your plate without really eating much of it. It's an old word, and an obscure one at that, which appears in an 1823 dictionary of Suffolk dialect (vital if you ever find yourself in Long Melford with a time machine).

> **PINGLE**. To eat a little, without appetite. 'I heen't no stummach for my wittels. I jest *pingle* a bit.'

Pingle should not be confused with *pinguid*, which means greasy, though if the food is too much the latter, it may cause the former. So if you were stuck with a bad cook in Antarctica you might pingle a pinguid penguin.

A bad cook is a crime against lunch and a sin against nature's bounty. The cow and the cabbage die for us, and the least a cook can do to reward their selfless sacrifice is to cook them well and give to their corpses an honourable marinade. To do otherwise is to be the very devil, and as the devil used to be known as *ruffin*, the old term for a bad cook was therefore:

COOK RUFFIN: The Devil of a Cook; or a very bad one. (1723)

A cook ruffin can turn the noblest beast in nature into a mere *kickshaw*, which was ruefully defined in Dr Johnson's dictionary as 'A dish so changed by the cookery that it can scarcely be known'. The word kickshaw is, in fact, a garbled version of the French *quelque chose*, which simply means 'something'. The worst restaurants of old London Town had heard the French term, wished to appear fine and Frenchified; but one must imagine that their food was as bad as their pronunciation. Some scholars take a reversed view and believe that kickshaw was a contemptuous term for French food, which was effete and enfeebled, as opposed to proper British fare, which was filled with roast beef and vigour.

Those who are, like the French, very particular about what they devour, have all sorts of lovely names. They are the *gastolaters* or stomach worshippers, they are the *ingurgitating belly-gods*. They are the *goinfres*, the *gullet-fanciers* and *golofers*. However, the finest phrase in the dictionary for such epicures is *turtle-eater*.

Turtles were well known to be the best food available to mankind before they became endangered and hard to find in the supermarket. But even in the eighteenth century to eat a turtle required a lot of money. First, you had to import the creatures alive and then have a special room built in your house to keep them in. You had to feed them on a leg of mutton every day. Then you had to have a special oven capacious enough to fit a whole turtle, and cooks specially trained in their execution and preparation. Then, of course, you had to have special turtle-eating clothes. In fact, it would be best at this point to turn to an account of a turtle feast written in 1755:

> Upon hearing the clock strike, he [the immensely wealthy host] rung his bell, and asked if his turtle cloaths were aired. While I was meditating on this new term, and, I confess unable to divine what it could mean, the servant brought in a coat and waistcoat, which my friend slipped on, and, folding them round his body like a nightgown, declared that, though they then hung so loose about him, by that time he had spoke with the turtle, he should stretch them as tight as a drum.

And once the turtle is on the table and the guests have arrived, those closest to it forget all good manners in order to obtain the finest parts. And those at the other end of the table?

> In vain did they send their plates, and solicit their share; the plunderers, who were now in possession of both the shells, were sensible to no call but that of their own appetites, and, till they had satisfied them, there was not one that would listen to anything else.

The taste of the turtle was so fine that it conquered all good manners, drained fortunes and jaded appetites. Even those who could not afford a turtle of their own could at least pretend that they were at a turtle feast. Thus the invention of *mock turtle soup*, which was simply a boiled calf's head. Those who were not obscenely rich were assured that this was the closest they would ever get to the true heaven of turtle-eating.

From all this, it should be easy to see why *turtle-eater* became a byword for those of the finest and most luxurious palate. It is, anyway, better than a *petecure*, which is modest cooking, or *rypophagy*, which means 'the eating of filth'. Rypophagy is actually a terribly useful word for insulting somebody's cookery without letting them know that you're doing it, as in: 'Thank you for such a large, and may I say rypophagous, meal. No, I mean it. I don't think I've ever eaten a meal of quite that quality before. You're a regular cook ruffin.'

Aftermath

There is a single word in the English language meaning 'a person given to remaining at table'. It is *residentarian*, and, so far as I can tell, it has been used only once, in 1680 by the writer of a rather dull religious tract who was complaining about those who sing hymns without really meaning them:

> The daily feaster, such as the Residentarians, whose legs can scarce bear about his Gross Corpulent Body, he sings, *My knees are weak through Fasting, and my Flesh faileth of Fatness.*
>
> Satan's Captive, who wallows in the Mire and Puddle of Sin and Iniquity, he sings, *O Lord, truly I am thy servant.*

But the mire and puddle of sin and iniquity is such a comfortable place, and good for one's digestion. It is a good place for belching, or *eructation*, to give it its more genteel name, and without a little after-lunch lounging one is liable to end up *wamblecropt* for the rest of the day.

Wamblecropt is the most exquisite word in the English language. Say it. Each syllable is intolerably beautiful.

Wamblecropt.

Wamblecropt gets its first mention in the *Abecedarium Anglico Latinum* of 1552, which you have doubtless read. It's a sort of early English-to-Latin dictionary. So if you were wondering what the Romans would call a 'Siege, jacques, bogard, or draught', it tells you that they are all *latrina*. It also tells you:

Wamble cropped *Stomachichus*

Wamble stomaked to be *Nauseo*

Wamblyng of stomake, or disposition, or will to vomit. *Nausea*

That ought to give you some idea, but if you want something more precise (or less Latinate) then the OED has *wamble* as 'a rolling or uneasiness of the stomach' and *wamblecropt* as being afflicted with and incapacitated by such wambling. So wamblecropt means queasy, only slightly stronger.

The odd thing about the word is that after a little citation from 1616 the wamblecropt goes into hiding and doesn't reappear until 1798 in America, where it remained. The *Massachusetts Spy* has the line, 'I feel a good deal womblecropped about dropping her acquaintance'. And that is almost the end of wamblecropt. It was revived here and there but always as a joke, an example of a dialect word, a mickey-take. For example, there was a humorous Canadian writer called Thomas Chandler Haliburton who wrote a (rather good) series of sketches in the persona of Sam Slick, who says of marriage that:

> The difference atween a wife and a sweetheart is near about as great as there is between new and hard cider: a man never tires of puttin' one to his lips, but makes plaguy wry faces at t'other. It makes me so kinder wamblecropt when I think on it, that I'm afeared to venture on matrimony at all.

Sam Slick uses the word, but I doubt that Haliburton did. It was fast disappearing down the chute of quaint dialect and all future uses are of the '"By jiminee I'll be wamblecropt", averred the blacksmith quaintly' variety.

Wambling, of the uncropt kind, survived far longer on these shores. Indeed, wambling was a standard activity of British stomachs right up to the late nineteenth century. Here are my three favourite examples:

> [My soul] can digest a monster without crudity, a sin as weighty as an elephant, and never wamble for it.
> Thomas Middleton, *A Game At Chess* (1624) (because I like the sin as big as an elephant)

> Vast fires subterranean … work and wamble in the bowels of the earth
> John Goad, *Astro-Meteorologica* (1686) (because I like the idea of the earth having indigestion)

> Yes faith have I [been in love], and have felt your flames and fires, and inclinations and wamblings.
> Thomas Betterton, *The Revenge* (1680) (because it's beautiful)

Incidentally, wamble can by extension mean to roll or stumble around and can be spelled with an O, making *womble*.

And nothing is so inclined to crop your wambles as the arrival of the bill. This is the dread moment when you hope that Sir Timothy Treat-All is a good residentarian. Otherwise, it may fall to you to waste yourself in *abligurition*. Abligurition is 'extravagant spending on food and drink' and is a terribly valuable word when it comes to filing expenses claims, especially as it has a rather legal ring to it. The wily business traveller could happily say that they had spent ten thousand pounds on conveyancing and abligurition without anybody in HR being any the wiser. It comes from the Latin word *abligurire* which meant 'to squander on dainties', and thus has the justification of antiquity.

The Romans were greedy fellows, but the ancient Greeks had no word for squandering money on long and luxurious lunches. They knew what to spend their ancient cash on. Instead of *abligurire*, they had the word *katapepaiderastekenai*, which meant 'squander your money on the love of beautiful boys'.

Chapter 9

2 p.m. – Returning to Work

Nap – phoning family members

⌒⌒⌒

Thank God for modern medicine. It was not until 1905 that *ergophobia* (the morbid fear of returning to work) was first identified and reported in the *British Medical Journal*. As yet there is no known cure, but doctors have been working on it, and may get back to working on it sometime soon.

There is something about a good lunch that quite cures one of the delusion that toil is ennobling. It frees one from the temptation to strive, to seek, to find and not to yield. Instead, one sees the immediate and practical necessity for a *nooningscaup*, which was the rest granted to the farm labourers of Yorkshire after a particularly laborious lunch. One might have imagined that a nooningscaup would occur at noon, and though that's correct, it should be noted that noon has moved backwards over the years. Noon was originally the ninth, or in Old English *non*, hour after dawn, which averages it out as three o'clock. Nobody is quite sure why noon moved backwards, but it did, leaving some odd words behind, one of which appears to be nooningscaup, which probably originally meant noon-song. Midday was therefore, of course, the sixth hour or *sexta hora* in Latin, from which we get *siesta*.

The world being what it is, appearances must be maintained and you ought to show your face back at the office before discreetly dozing off in your cubicle. This may be difficult, especially if your lunch hour ended up being *sesquihoral*, or an hour and a half long.

You could delay your return to work and just wander about. You could even go out for a *doundrins* or afternoon drinking session. But your absence might be noticed, and the Scots have a word for that sort of thing (or at least they did in Victorian Aberdeenshire):

> **CAUSEY-WEBS** A person is said to make *causey-webs*, who neglects his or her work, and is too much on the street.

An efficient way to make causey-webs is to *gongoozle*. Gongoozling has the benefit of being a ridiculous-sounding word that manages to contain *gone*, *goose* and *ooze* all in one. In fact, it's probably a portmanteau of two ancient dialect terms: *gawn* meaning 'stare curiously' and *gooze* meaning 'stare aimlessly'; but its technical meaning, set for eternity in the OED, is to stare at canals. This is one of those words that must cause even the most avid dictionary reader to stop and wonder to himself: Why?

The term gongoozler is first recorded in a glossary of canal terminology:

> **Gongoozler**, an idle and inquisitive person who stands staring for prolonged periods at anything out of the common. This word is believed to have its origin in the Lake District of England.

There is still a small canal in Ulverston, but it is closed, which must render the lives of the true and native gongoozlers even less eventful than before. Nonetheless, it is as pleasant a way of spending an afternoon as any, and there are always the ducks.

But if canals don't interest you, the thing to do is to head back to your workplace for a nap. The best way to do this is to *snudge* along to your desk. Everybody snudges along now and then, even if they don't know that they're doing it. Nathan Bailey's *Universal Etymological Dictionary* (1721) defines it thus:

> **To SNUDGE along**: to walk looking downward, and poring, as though the Head was full of Business.

Nobody will interrupt you if you snudge, especially if you use the modern prop of the mobile phone, which can be studied with undistractable intensity. Indeed, a really good snudger could probably just snudge around the office for years without being caught and end up drawing a handsome pension, all for having learned how to furrow his brow in just the right way. However, permanently snudging along would probably work havoc with your feet and so it's best to get back to your desk where you can have a good *rizzle*.

Rizzle is a mysterious word that had a sudden vogue in late nineteenth-century America and then disappeared. It appeared in several terribly respectable medical journals and might have had the same success as ergophobia, as doctors of that lost and lovely era were clearly civilised chaps and not the stern fun-spoilers who prowl around the hospitals of today telling you not to smoke or eat turtles. Here is a description of *rizzling* taken from the American *Medical Bulletin* of 1890:

Do you rizzle every day? Do you know how to rizzle? One of the swell doctors in town says that it is the most wonderful aid to perfect health.

'I masticate my food very thoroughly at dinner,' he says, 'and make sure to have my family or friends entertain me with bright talk and plenty of fun. After dinner it is understood that I am going to rizzle. How do I do it? I retire to my study, and having darkened the room, I light a cigar, sit down and perform the operation.

'How to describe it I don't know, but it is a condition as nearly like sleep as sleep is like death. It consists in doing absolutely nothing.

'I close my eyes and try to stop all action of the brain. I think of nothing. It only takes a little practice to be able to absolutely stifle the brain.

'In that delightful condition I remain at least ten minutes, sometimes twenty. That is the condition most helpful to digestion, and it is that which accounts for the habit animals have of sleeping after eating. I would rather miss a fat fee than that ten minutes' rizzle every day.'

People are liable to notice if you pull down all the blinds and start smoking a cigar at your desk, and if they don't you can be sure that you are working in a very superior sort of office. However, in the late Victorian world it would have been considered, quite rightly, a medical necessity.

Sometimes, though, rizzling is not enough. Emptiness of the mind may be fine for the enthusiast of meditation, but what of those who really need a good nap and don't have a cigar to hand? These people may now *sloom*.

Sloom is a beautiful word because you almost know what it means without needing to be told. The *Oxford English Dictionary* defines it as a 'gentle sleep or slumber', inadvertently letting us know that all the best sleeping words begin with SL. This was a point not lost upon the alliterative poets of Middle English, who could write lovely lines like:

Slipped upon a sloumbe sleep

There was even a proper set of rules on how to have your after-dinner medieval sloom. The fourteenth century was teeming with courtesy books, which were rather like self-help manuals for nervous knights. These would tackle all of the important subjects like how to make your armour shine, how to address a dragon, and how to have a nap after lunch.

Whole men of what age or complexion so ever they be of, should take their natural rest and sleep in the night: and to eschew meridial sleep. But and [if] need shall compel a man to sleep after his meat: let him make a pause, and than let him stand and lean and sleep against a cupboard, or else let him sit upright in a chair and sleep.

Sleeping against a cupboard is nearly impossible, and, worse, much more likely to get you noticed. So sit in your chair and *streke*, which is to say stretch out all your limbs. Now, rest some worthy-looking file of papers with one end on your stomach and the other on the edge of the desk, let the tip of your chin rest upon your neck and very subtly sloom, and dream of being a knight errant.

Intermission

Feeling refreshed? Splendid. You may draw the curtains and extinguish your cigar, for rizzling and slooming are over and there may be nothing for it but to do some work. What are your *facienda*? Your list of things that you must get done? They must be tackled one faciendum at a time, of course; you wouldn't want to strain something. But facienda there must be. Otherwise somebody will notice and you'll be out of a job and forced to gongoozle all day, which would probably become rather dull, canal traffic being so much reduced from its day of hey.

A quick phone call

Perhaps you should turn to your personal facienda, especially as you've only just woken up, and perform your familial duties by calling a relative. Relatives like to be telephoned. Nobody knows why, but they do. Now seems as good a time as any, and you never know when people will be drawing up their wills. So, just to be helpful, here are all the words you'll need to love your family.

Uxorious: Excessively fond of one's wife. It should be noted that wives rarely put any stress on the *excessively* part of that definition, feeling correctly that whatever fondness they get is too little. Uxorious also has the splendid little cousin word *uxorilocal*, which means 'of a husband living in the vicinity of his wife's relatives'. Whether this is a good or bad thing is disputed.

Maritorious: Excessively fond of one's husband. This is, for some reason, a much rarer word than uxorious. Indeed, few people have ever heard of it. This may be because its only notable appearance in English literature is in the pithy statement: 'Dames maritorious ne'er were meritorious.'

Philadelphian: Loving your brother. Alternatively this can mean from the city of Philadelphia, which was named after the virtue of brotherly (*adelphian*) love (*philos*). This should not be confused with *philodelphian*, which would mean loving dolphins.

I have never found a word for loving your sister. This may be significant.

Matriotic: This is a usefully abstract word for doting on your mother, although it can also simply mean nostalgic love for one's old school or university. There are other words for loving one's mother, but they generally have some connection to an uncouth fellow called Oedipus who was unlucky and is dead.

Philopater: One who loves his father or his country. The true philopater can be recognised by their tendency to *patrizate*, or to take after or imitate one's father (again, not like that evil Oedipus).

Philoprogenitive: Loving one's offspring. This was, originally, a phrenological term and referred to a philoprogenitive bump on the skull.

Materteral: Relating to an aunt. Amazingly this word never appears in the works of P.G. Wodehouse.

Avuncular: Relating to an uncle, more specifically a maternal uncle. There's an even more curious and useless term:

the *avunculate*, which means maternal uncles considered as a group.[1]

It's a little thing, but a phone call to a loved one can make all the difference. Think of how much pain could have been avoided if King Lear had only called Cordelia from the blasted heath, or if Odysseus had texted Penelope to say that he would be late, or had Romeo picked up the phone to hear the sweet sound of his wife's voice saying, 'Hi, I'm in the crypt'.

If you are to use Alexander Graham Bell's product, which is to say the blower, you should, in all courtesy, use it as he would have wished; and Dr Bell insisted that all phone calls should begin with the words 'Ahoy, ahoy'. Nobody knows why he insisted this – he had no connection to the navy – but insist he did and started every phone call that way. Nobody else did, and it was at the suggestion of his great rival Edison that people took to saying 'Hello'. This seems unfair.

Telephones improved greatly over the course of the twentieth century and went, in terms of the reproduction of sound, from a distorted and distant voice to a clear and ringing intimacy. Such was the improvement that we all decided we needed a new challenge and switched to mobile telephones, which give you the splendidly retro feeling of crackly lines, broken connections and Too Few Bars.

Soldiers and pilots have been dealing with such precarious lines for years and have developed a thing they call Voice Procedure that eliminates all sorts of annoyances. For example,

---

[1] And, in case you need them, the words for murdering all these would be *uxoricide, mariticide, fratricide, sororicide, matricide, parricide* and *filicide*.

if you are a coastguard radioing the captain of a sinking ship you don't want to spend ten minutes having a conversation that goes 'Can you hear me?' 'I can hear you, can you hear me?' 'I can't hear what you said. Did you say you could hear me?' Quite aside from the fact that a hundred souls might be lost beneath the angry waves, it's just plain annoying. So, instead of saying 'So sorry, I can't quite make you out. Could you repeat that?', coastguards just go: 'Say again.' This is a practice that could usefully be applied to modern mobile communications that are cursed with a Bad Line. Here are the important ones:

Roger means 'I can hear you perfectly well, granny'. This is because 'roger' and 'received' both begin with an R. Incidentally, *roger* can also mean 'have sexual intercourse', which makes the technical terms *roger that* and *roger so far* rather amusing. (*Roger* can also mean 'an itinerant beggar pretending to be a poor scholar from Oxford or Cambridge' but nobody knows why.)

Wilco (short for **will co**mply) means 'Absolutely, granny, I shall remember to wrap up warm'.

Copy means 'Yes, I heard what you just said. There's no need to repeat it.'

Reading you five: 'Yes, the line is perfectly good from my end.'

Wait out means 'I've no idea, can I call you back sometime?'

And, most importantly, all chitchat about the weather or instructions on which bus to take to the pub tonight should be prefixed with *Securité!*, which means 'I have important meteorological, navigational or safety information to pass on'.

Got all that? Good. So a typical phone call to your dear old mother might go something like this:

> 'Ahoy, ahoy! Just feeling matriotic and thought I'd give you a call.'
> 'Darling! So lovely to copy that.'
> 'Roger that. How are things?'
> 'Securité! Securité! We've had such glorious weather this morning that I was out in the garden, but then Securité! Securité! it began to drizzle a bit so I came inside. Now, when are you going to come up and visit us?'
> 'Wait out.'
> 'It's been five years.'

Click. Phone call finished. Family obligations and filial piety complete. As it says in the Ten Commandments: 'Honour thy father and thy mother that thy days may be long in the land of the Lord.' It's the only commandment with a promise.

Chapter 10

3 p.m. – Trying to Make Others Work

Finding them – shouting at them

৩৵৵

If you follow learning you shall learn more each day. If you follow the Way you shall do less each day. You shall do less and less until you do nothing at all. And, if you do nothing at all, there is nothing that is left undone.

The Tao Te Ching of Lao Tzu, fifth century BC

So far I have been assuming that you are a subordinate, a mere Israelite slaving and sweating for some cruel taskmaster, and have provided you with the words necessary for workshy *lolly-gagging*. This is, perhaps, unfair, and I may have underestimated you. You could well be a captain of industry, a tycoon, a big shot, a *buzz-wig*, a *king-fish*, a *mob-master*, a *satrapon*, a *celestial*, a *top-hatter*, a *tall boy*, or a Fat Controller. If you are any or all of these, work avoidance is exactly the other way round: you must prowl around your business empire finding people to whom to delegate your toils, and you require the words with which to do it.

You must get your lazy *lolpoops* and *loobies* – your staff who are not operating as productive units of humanity – and scream

Imshi! at them, a Second World War expression meaning 'Get to work!'

Finding them

But first you must find them, and this is going to be a problem if your staff are *michers*, a micher being, according to Dr Johnson's dictionary, 'A lazy loiterer, who skulks about in corners and by-places, and keeps out of sight; a hedge creeper'. A *hedge creeper* is, of course, 'A hedge-thief, skulker under hedges, pitiful rascal' – according to Farmer's *Slang and its Analogues*, anyway.

The first thing to do is check under all the hedges in the office, a brief pursuit unless you manage a hedge fund. Having dealt with the hedge creepers, you must then turn your attention to the *latibulaters*, latibulate meaning 'hide in a corner'. In fact, you could save yourself some time by merely posting signs in every corner of the office saying NO LATIBULATION in big red letters. This may not solve the problem completely, though, as hardened latibulaters deprived of their corners may *incloacate*, or conceal themselves in a lavatory. Incloacation is not a common problem, but it was on the charge sheet of a seventeenth-century outlaw who was said to have 'incloacated himself privily'. Incloacaters are probably the hardest michers to deal with, and the best way to flush them out is to make the lavatories as unpleasant as possible. This is easily and subtly achieved by spraying the necessary room with *mercaptans*, one or more of the several stinking compounds in the sulphydryl group, or, to put it another way, the thing that smells in shit.

Shouting at them

Once all your *chasmophiles* – or lovers of nooks and crannies – have been beaten back to their desks and cubbyholes, you should give them a good earful. However, your reprimands must be chosen with the care befitting the dignity of an executive like you. You may be stern or soft, so long as you are memorable enough that your rockets stick in their memory, as it were. That way you shouldn't have to admonish anybody more than once a week or so. There was a don at Oxford University in the seventeenth century whose insults were considered so exquisite that they merit a whole paragraph in Aubrey's very brief *Brief Life* of him. His name was Dr Ralph Kettell and his ...

> ... fashion was to goe up and down the college, and peepe in at the key-holes to see whether the boyes did follow their bookes or no [...] When he scolded at the idle young boies of his colledge, he used these names, viz. *Turds*, *Tarrarags* (these were the worst sort, rude raskells), *Rascal-Jacks*, *Blindcinques*, *Scobberlotchers* (these did no hurt, were sober, but went idleing about the grove with their hands in their pocketts, and telling the number of trees there, or so).

These might seem to be enough, but they clearly weren't, as Aubrey also mentions that:

> Upon Trinity Sunday he would commonly preach at the Colledge, whither a number of the scholars of other howses would come, to laugh at him.

So you must, in your scolding, rise above even the invention of Dr Kettell. You could try resorting to John Florio's 1598 *Worlde of Wordes* and go for:

A shite-rags: an idle, lazie, loobie fellow

… but this may get you in trouble. To be honest, there are any number of words for layabouts, loafers, lingerers and *lurdans*. You might want to save time by just shouting at all of them at once, in which case you will need to know that the correct collective noun is a *lounge* of idlers. However, it might be more interesting to up the philosophical stakes by bringing in the concept of the *drogulus*.

The drogulus was invented as a purely theoretical concept by the British philosopher A.J. Ayer. Ayer is a chap who deserves everybody's respect and time, if not for his thought, then at least for the fact that he once, at the age of 77, stopped Mike Tyson from attacking a young model called Naomi Campbell. It was at a party in New York, and when Ayer got in the way Mike Tyson asked him: 'Do you know who the fuck I am? I'm the heavyweight champion of the world.' To which Ayer replied: 'And I am the former Wykeham Professor of Logic. We are both pre-eminent in our field. I suggest that we talk about this like rational men.' Meanwhile, Miss Campbell had slipped away.

But to return to the drogulus: this fascinating little speculative creature was invented in a less glamorous argument in 1949 when Ayer was debating with a priest about meaningful and meaningless statements. Ayer contended that a statement could be meaningful only if you could state what would prove that it was true or false. So 'God exists' would be a meaningful statement only if you could say definitively what would make you believe or disbelieve it. Ayer invented the idea of the drogulus, which is a creature that has no discernible effect whatsoever on anything.

> And you say, 'Well how am I to tell if it's there or not?' And I say, 'There's no way of telling. Everything's just the same if it's there or it's not there. But the fact is it's there.'

Drogulus has remained a term of speculative epistemological philosophy, but it could easily be imported into the repertoire of management-speak. For what better insult to a lazy employee than 'You drogulus!' It sounds a bit like *dog* and a bit like *useless*, but if your subordinate went crying to an employment tribunal, they would probably be rather impressed with your erudition and say with A.J. Ayer: 'Everything is just the same if you're there or you're not there. But the fact is you're there.'

All this, of course, assumes that there is Something To Be Done. And if there is not something to be done then it is your duty as manager to cover the fact up. This has been the central point of leadership since leadership began and there are all sorts of cunning and inventive manoeuvres. For example, on 1 April junior employees used to be sent out to buy *pigeon milk* for their masters. Every shopkeeper would direct them onwards to somewhere just round the corner and they could wander around town all day on this *sleeveless errand*.

On exactly the same basis, modern recruits to the British Army are often sent by their commanding officer to get *the keys to the indoor tank park*. Indeed, the futility of war is as nothing to the futility of basic training, where the old rule is that if it doesn't move you should paint it and that if it does you should salute it.

Even once you have sent your employees running around milking pigeons, you must still watch them like hawks in case they are merely *eye-servants* and *lip-labourers*.

> EYESERVANT. n.s. [*eye* and *servant.*] A servant that works only while watched ...
> Servants, obey in all things your masters; not with *eye-service*, as men pleasers, but in singleness of heart. Cor. I ii.22

> LIP-LABOUR. n.s. [*lip* and *labour.*] Action of the lips without concurrence of the mind; words without sentiments.
> Christ calleth your Latyne howres idlenesse, hypocresye, moche bablynge, and *lyppe-laboure*. Bale, *Yet a Course &c* (1543)

Eye-servants are even worse than those incloacated chasmo-philes mentioned earlier, because you think they're working when in fact they are napping, phoning their friends, tweet-ing, texting, booking their faces, indulging their *oniomania* (or compulsion to buy stuff) on the Internet, or otherwise *ploiter-ing*, which is to say pretending to work when they are not. Such people are leeches upon the healthy limbs of business and must be salted accordingly.

Dressing down

At this point, you may be called upon to summon them to *a meeting without coffee*. This is an immensely useful term

invented in the British Ministry of Defence. It combines gentle-
ness of phrasing with a subtle and malevolent menace. On the
international stage the Ministry of Defence will go and organise
naval manoeuvres or missile tests right next to whatever impish
country they want to intimidate. Internally, they achieve exactly
the same effect by mentioning a meeting without coffee. It works
like this. A senior officer's secretary will phone up a subordinate
to arrange a meeting. The subordinate will say something along
the lines of, 'Oh, that's splendid. I'm terribly excited about our
new initiatives on installing tea-makers in British Army tanks,[1]
and I'd like to discuss the possibility ...' But here the secretary
will cut them off with the dread words: 'Actually, this is a meeting without coffee.'

It's an easy and friendly thing for the secretary to say, but
the subordinate knows what it means. Their opinion will not be
asked. They will not be smiled at. They will not even be allowed
to sit down and sip a thoughtful cup of the brown stuff. They
will stand there and be shouted at until their feet are sore and
their ears *tintinnabulate*. A good, proper military carpeting. And
the beauty of it is that the dread felt on the part of the subordinate as they pencil the meeting meekly into their diary, as they
fail to sleep the night before, as they spend all morning fretting
and practising excuses – that dread is the real punishment. It is
psychological trench warfare.

But should you be so cruel? Would it not be better to organise a caring and sharing office environment where everybody
feels valued? No, it would not. I refer you to Machiavelli.

---

[1] I am, of course, making this example up. British Army tanks all contain tea-
making facilities as it stands. Really.

It has been asked whether it is better to be loved than feared, or feared than loved. I am of the opinion that both are necessary; but as it is not an easy task to unite them, and we must determine on one or the other, I think the latter (to be feared) is the safest. Men, it must be allowed, are generally ungrateful, fickle, timid, dissembling, and self-interested; so much so, that confer on them a benefit they are entirely yours; they offer you, as I have already said, their wealth, their blood, their lives, and even their own offspring, when the occasion for any of them is distant; but should it present itself, they will revolt against you.

Any questions? Good. Now that your meeting without coffee has been arranged with the eye-serving drogulus, the next step is to work out exactly what you are going to say. It's always good to start with something ear-catching, and, as the executive self-help books suggest, to learn from history's greatest managers. When Ghengis Khan seized Bukhara he gathered all the city's most prominent citizens to kneel before him and began his pep talk thus:

I am the punishment of God. If you had not committed great sins, God would not have sent a punishment like me upon you.

Change 'punishment' to 'line manager' and you have your opening. Ghengis could have saved a lot of time by using the word *theomeny*, which means wrath of God, but we will let that pass. Now that you've softened them up and established the tone of the meeting (and hidden any stray cafetieres) you can press home your advantage by shrieking the dread words: 'You are a *purple dromedary!*'

Pause for a while to let this sink in; it is a terrible thing for anyone to learn that they are a purple dromedary. The pain is particularly acute if you have not read *A New Dictionary of the Terms Ancient and Modern of the Canting Crew*, where they translate:

You are a purple Dromedary – You are a Bungler or a dull Fellow

If you're feeling particularly alliterative you can add *drumbledore* to dromedary, for, although the former is usually applied to a clumsy insect, it can also mean a clumsy, incompetent individual.

Now that their dromedarian nature has been exposed, you can pin them down with any of the other words that English has produced for the incurable incompetent: *maflard, puzzlepate, shaffles, foozler, juffler, blunkerkin* or *batie-bum*. Or if you feel that the work of selecting words is beneath the dignity of a director like you, you can just copy Shakespeare, who provided a handy cut-out-and-memorise passage in *King Lear*, where Kent calls Oswald:

A knave; a rascal; an eater of broken meats; a base, proud, shallow, beggarly, three-suited, hundred-pound, filthy, worsted-stocking knave; a lily-livered, action-taking knave, a whore-son, glass-gazing, super-serviceable finical rogue; one-trunk-inheriting slave; one that wouldst be a bawd, in way of good service, and art nothing but the composition of a knave, beggar, coward, pandar, and the son and heir of a mongrel bitch: one whom I will beat into clamorous whining, if thou deniest the least syllable of thy addition.

Shakespeare saw that simply piling up personal abuse is much more effective than trying to be clever. And, in case you were wondering:

Finical = excessively fastidious
Super-serviceable = Officious
Action-taking = litigious

Incidentally, the OED lists this as the very first citation for 'son of a bitch', demonstrating what a debt we owe to the Bard.

Your employee is probably now weeping and quivering and appealing for mercy. Show none. If they plead and beg, just say in a deep and dismal voice 'Gabos', and shake your head.

Gabos (or G.A.B.O.S.) is an acronym for Game Ain't Based On Sympathy. The game in question is the frolicsome world of gangland Miami, where the enthusiastic and endearingly territorial *narcotraficantes* refer to their lives, their code of conduct, their retail activities and occasional tiffs as The Game. Unlike cricket, this game has no central authority, book of laws, professional umpires, or even an equivalent of *Wisden*. In fact, nobody is quite sure what The Game is based on at all, yet all agree that the Game Ain't Based On Sympathy, and that kicking a gangster when they're down, or indeed popping a cap into their ass while so prostrated, is thoroughly licit. It would appear that the term is merely the beginning of a long process of elimination that will eventually lead to the discovery of firm foundations for The Game and thus clear up all the confusion.

This lack of sympathy with the plucky underdog was shortened into an acronym some time in the early years of this century and then made popular by rappers and documentaries.

Thus it is no longer the preserve of Miamians, and is now, I am told, part of the common parlance of the British House of Commons. The use of the word gabos in the office will give you a rakish, gangstery air that is bound to increase the productivity of your terrified subordinates or 'soldiers' as you may now call them.

You may finish off your carpeting by threatening to *rightsize* them. Rightsizing is the euphemistic way of saying *downsizing* which is the euphemistic way of saying *streamlining* which is the euphemistic way of saying that you'll sack the whole sorry lot of them any day now. This saves on confusion because the verb 'to sack' has several different meanings listed in the dictionary, including

> **Sack**: To put (a person) in a sack to be drowned.
> 1425 *Rolls of Parl.* IV. 298/2 Ye said Erle lete sakke hym forth-with, and drounyd him in Thamyse.

Oh for the heady days of real line management. Once you have herded everybody to their desks, shouted at a few people, and put the fear of God and unemployment into every purple dromedary, there is nothing much more for a good manager to do beyond playing golf and drawing a salary. And, besides, it's time for tea.

Chapter 11

4 p.m. – Tea

ᠵᡐᡐᡐᠵ

There's an odd thing that though an English lord might have a cup of *tea*, the working classes are as likely to have a cup of *cha*. In this they are correct. 'Cha' is the original aristocratic Mandarin name for the infusion of *Camellia sinensis*, 'tea' is merely the term used in Fuchau, the coastal province from which the stuff was shipped to Europe. So it should be cha if you're feeling posh, and tea only if you're feeling particularly raffish and filled with *nostalgie de la boue*.[1]

The first great treatise on tea, by the eighth-century writer Lu Yu, was called the *Ch'a Ching* or Classic of Cha. The name *cha*, along with the plant, was imported into Japan, where the true lover of a good cuppa is not merely a tea enthusiast, but a follower of *Chado*: the Way of Tea (*do*, pronounced *doh*, is the word for 'way').

Chado is the mystic and magical practice of drinking tea in order to achieve spiritual enlightenment, and is a lot more fun than fasting or self-flagellation. Any particular instance of Chado is called *chanoyu*, which translated literally means 'tea's hot water'. However, it is difficult for our debased Western

---

[1] This is a French term meaning 'homesickness for mud', which refers to those of the upper classes longing for the gritty suffering of the lower.

minds, filled with the cheap spiritual gratification of the teabag and electric kettle, to appreciate the obscure Oriental mystery of tea.

It is a common piece of wisdom in the lands of the rising sun that 'Zen and tea are one and the same'. This may lead you to believe that you can practise zen merely by sipping at a cup of Rosie Lea, but this is not so. The great tea-master Shuko taught that you could not drink tea unless your mind was completely pure, a proposition I have disproved by experiment.

The greatest master of Chado was Rikyu, in the sixteenth century, whose skill with a teapot was so great that his overlord became jealous and ordered him to commit *seppuku*, or ritual suicide. Rikyu made what is meant to have been the finest damn cup of tea in history, after which he broke the teacup and obediently fell upon his sword.

In English we do have some equivalents to the idea of Chado. The poet Percy Bysshe Shelley was expelled from Oxford for writing a tract called *The Necessity of Atheism*, signed 'Thro' deficiency of proof, AN ATHEIST'. But in private he freely admitted that he was a *theist*, by which he meant nothing in the way of religion, only that he was addicted to tea (French *thé*). Theism became as popular a religion as England has ever known. In 1886 an article appeared in *The Lancet* saying:

America and England are the two countries afflicted most with the maladies arising from the excessive consumption of tea. Individuals may suffer in a variety of ways. It is customary to speak of acute, sub acute, and chronic 'theism' – a form that has no connection with theological matters. It is possible to be a 'theic' by profession, or a 'theic' by passion [...] There is hardly a morbid symptom which may not be traceable to tea as its cause.

Given that the love of tea is both a religious rite and a narcotic need, it is unsurprising that all sorts of terrible names have been invented for badly made tea. For example, tea that is too weak may be cursed with the name of *cat-lap*, *husband's tea*, *maiden's pee*, and *blash*. Indeed, one who has made the tea too weak may be said to have *drowned the miller* for reasons that nobody is quite sure of.

The opposite of such watery nonsense is strong tea, tea that blows your mind and wakes you up. Thus British servicemen of the Second World War would refer to good strong tea as *gunfire*, on the basis that it had the same enlivening effect upon the senses as coming under attack from the enemy.

Nor is this caffeinism a recent development. According to an utterly reliable Japanese legend, there was a monk named Bodhidharma who had sworn to spend nine years staring at a blank bit of wall. Why he would want to do this is not recorded, but it was considered terribly holy and nobody seems to have mentioned to him that it might be a waste of time. The story goes that after a mere five years he got tired and dozed off. When he woke up the wall was still very much there but, nonetheless, Bodhidharma felt awfully ashamed and, to make sure that it never happened again and he wouldn't miss a moment of the fun, he cut off his own eyelids and chucked them on the ground. The eyelids germinated and sprouted and from them grew the very first tea plant. Bodhidharma decided to make an infusion from the leaves (presumably without taking his eyes off the wall – I've never been able to get this point clear) and thus was made the first cup of tea. The caffeine contained in it was enough to keep him alert for the next four years.

So let us get to the making. While the kettle is thrumbling away you must first choose your brew. Here is a quick reference guide to the various etymologies of tea.

Charles Grey, 2nd **Earl Grey**, was a great man. He became an MP at the age of 22, seduced the Duchess of Devonshire, was Prime Minister of Britain from 1830 to 1844, and passed the Great Reform Act and the abolition of slavery. But he is chiefly remembered for being fond of tea flavoured with bergamot oil, a fondness that was leapt upon by tea merchants eager to associate their wares with such a chap. Lady Grey is a figment of a tea merchant's caffeinated imagination. There was, of course, a real Lady Grey, but she was too busy having sixteen children to bother about bergamots.

Lapsang Souchong (or *lāpǔshān xiǎozhǒng*) means 'small plant from Lapu Mountain'. A rather unreliable story says that an army arrived and wanted their tea, but as the crop was still damp it was dried quickly over fires built from pine trees, hence the smoky flavour.

Ceylon was the old name for the island of Sri Lanka. It comes from the Sanskrit *Sinhala*, which means 'blood of a lion', which is odd as there are no lions in Sri Lanka.

Assam means either 'unequal' or 'unequalled'. If the former, then it's probably due to the mountainous terrain of this far north-eastern state of India; if the latter, then it's due to the ancient rulers of the area who thought themselves peerless.

Darjeeling comes from the Tibetan *dojeling*, which means 'diamond island'. This is down to the practice there of Vajrayana Buddhism. *Vajra* can mean diamond and so *Vajrayana* is often translated as 'diamond vehicle'. However, there is another story that Darjeeling is named after a particular stone that people used to meet at to gossip, called the *Taji-lung* in the native language. This latter etymology is rather appropriate as tea has always been intimately connected with gossip, even in English. Some used to call it *chatter broth*, others *scandal broth*, as in this lament of a pious farmer in 1801:

> ... we never have any tea but on Sundays, for it will not do for a hardworking family, and many of our neighbours call it *Scandal broth*.

The Victorians, in a rare fit of simplicity, just had:

> BITCH, tea; 'a bitch party,' tea drinking.

Anyway, the kettle should have boiled now and the tea should be drawing. It must not do so for too long or it will be *overdrawn* and *potty* – which is to say, tasting of the teapot. So grasp the handle of the teapot (technically called the *boul*, which is also the name for the little finger holes in scissors) and pour the bitch into a teacup.

Skeuomorphs

The handle of the common or garden teacup is a classic example of a *skeuomorph*. In the nineteenth century, when photography was still in nappies, exposure times were so long that people who were walking would be blurred. They would have ghosts flowing out behind them. It was this that introduced the idea in paintings and drawings that movement could be indicated by lines flying out behind a moving object. Photography changed our visual ideas and that changed representations in other mediums. The viewer looks at a blurred drawing and thinks: 'Ah, the chap's running. I know that because of the technological failings of photography.' Think about it: have you ever actually seen a runner with lines coming out of their back?

There's a technical term for this: it's *skeuomorphic*. A skeuomorph is a technological limitation that is deliberately imitated even when it's no longer necessary. My digital camera has a little loudspeaker that emits a clicking noise when I take a photograph, just like an old mechanical camera.

Once upon a time there were teacups whose handles you might reasonably fit your fingers through. They were handles that you could, well, handle. But now they remain purely as skeuomorphic decoration, a mere memory of usefulness.

Now that the tea is ready and piping hot, it's time to summon your fellow *thermopotes* (or drinkers of hot drinks). You could do this with the rather dull shout of 'Tea's up', but for a bit of tropical allure there's nothing like this entry in an eighteenth-century dictionary:

> CONGO. Will you lap your congo with me? Will you drink tea with me?

You may add some *moo juice*, but as Fielding said: 'Love and scandal are the best sweeteners of tea.'

Reading your future

And once the day's gossip is done, and the cha is all gone, it remains only to check the tea leaves to see what the future holds. Tea-leaf reading is called *tasseography* and there is, so far as I can tell, only one major work on the subject: *Tea-Cup Reading and Fortune-Telling by Tea Leaves* by 'A Highland Seer' (1920). It contains a dictionary, or at least a table of 'Symbols and significations', which is practically the same thing. The idea is to look at the tea leaves left in the cup and see if you can discern any familiar shapes. Here is a brief selection of the ones I consider most urgent:

AIRCRAFT, unsuccessful projects.

BADGER, long life and prosperity as a bachelor.

CANNON, good fortune.

CAR (MOTOR), and CARRIAGE, approaching wealth, visits from friends.

DONKEY, a legacy long awaited.

GRASSHOPPER, a great friend will become a soldier.

KANGAROO, a rival in business or love.

KETTLE, death.

PARROT, a sign of emigration for a lengthy period.

UMBRELLA, annoyance and trouble.

YEW-TREE indicates the death of an aged person who will leave his possessions to the consultant.

ZEBRA, travel and adventure in foreign lands.

Chapter 12

5 p.m. – Actually Doing Some Work

Panicking – deadlines – giving up – stealing from your employer – leaving

❧

We are now approaching the end of the working day, and I don't mean to sound beastly, but it may be time to stop fudgeling and ploitering and actually do some work.

As five o'clock strikes you may well think wistfully of how you are missing out on your *cinqasept*. This French term may usefully be pondered (if only from a distance) for the light it throws on the French nation and their working practices as a whole. A cinqasept is literally a 'five till seven', but in French reality it means:

> A visit to a mistress or a brothel, traditionally made between five and seven p.m.

It's that word 'traditionally' that tells you all you need to know about Gallic morals. Oh, to be French! But it's too late now – you have an hour left at work and, so far as I can recall, you have achieved next to nothing. You must therefore attempt to fit a whole *dieta* (or day's work) into one measly hour of insane, *betwattled* toil. The end times are upon us.

Theologically speaking, we are in work's *eschaton*, which is the correct term for the rumpus that precedes the end of the world. If you're being very strict about things an apocalypse is not the end of the world, it is merely a *vision* of the eschaton. So The Apocalypse of Saint John the Divine, commonly known as the Book of Revelation, is just that: a revelation, or apocalypse, of what will happen when God finally calls time on this sorry mess we call existence. Viewed from this rigorous linguistic perspective, *Apocalypse Now* is a much less worrying title.

So to work! Time is ticking away and if we're going to get anything done we can't think about cinqasepts and revelations. We must get down to a proper *fit of the clevers*, as Sir Walter Scott's maids allegedly described a sudden burst of activity.

The Russians have a particularly wonderful word for such a work schedule: they call it *shturmovshchina*, and it is a word so useful that it might even be worthwhile remembering how to spell it. It is the practice of working frantically just before a deadline, having not done anything for the last month. The first element means 'storm' or 'assault', the second is a derogatory suffix.

Shturmovshchina originated in the Soviet Union. Factories would be given targets and quotas and other such rot by the state, but they often weren't given any raw materials. So they would sit around with their feet up and their tools down waiting until the necessaries arrived, and it was only when the deadline was knocking at the door and the gulag beckoned that they would panic, grab whatever was to hand, and do a really shoddy, half-arsed heap of work, or *shturmovshchina*. It's an excellent and easily usable word that should be included in the Special Skills section of any good CV.

Hermann Inclusus, or Hermann the Recluse, could be said to have engaged in a Satanic shturmovshchina. Hermann lived in the thirteenth century in Podlazice in the middle of Bohemia (which is now the Czech Republic, approximately). But Hermann was not like other monks praying and fasting and living a life of virtuous virginity. Hermann could never quite get the hang of virtue. Hermann the Recluse was an Evil Monk.

Nobody knows how evil Hermann was or in what particular specialities of evil he excelled, but it was quite enough to attract the notice of the other monks in the monastery, who decided that he was quite beyond any normal redemption or punishment and decided to *immure* him, which is to say that they put him in a room and then built a wall where the door had once been. This done they settled down, like good Christians, to let him starve to death.

Of course, Hermann Inclusus didn't want to die; he had all sorts of extra evil things he wanted to do and felt that he was being cut off in the prime of his sin. So he did a deal that involved writing a book to expiate his sins, although nobody seems to be very clear on how the deal was done or with whom.

This notion of writing as repentance was considered less odd at the time than it now appears. Atonement before the Lord is not included in modern publishing contracts, not even the very generous ones, but in the Middle Ages it was considered a practically automatic part of the system of royalties. For example, Oderic Vitalis (1075–1142), in his *Historia Ecclesiastica*, recounts a story about a monk who was surprisingly sinful, but also a very devoted scribe. When he died they counted up all the words that he had ever written and found that they outnumbered all the sins that he had ever committed, by a total of one. He therefore went to heaven.

So, Hermann the Recluse struck a deal whereby he could expiate his guilt by writing the biggest book in the whole wide world in a single night. He set to work, but like many writers who signed their contract thinking that it would be easy, he discovered the deadline charging towards him like a herd of elephants. He then struck a second deal, this one with the Devil (I told you that Hermann the Recluse was an evil monk). The Devil agreed to help him write the book, but only in exchange for Hermann's soul. Deal done, the book was produced in a single night, after which Hermann tried to strike a third deal giving him forgiveness and salvation, this time with the Virgin Mary, who, I suppose, happened to be around. However, just before he could sign on the dotted line, he died and went to Hell.

There are historians and cynics who question the absolute accuracy and veracity of the stories above, but no writer who has ever worked to a deadline would doubt a word of it.

Anyway, the book that was produced survives to this day. It's called the Codex Gigas and is kept in the National Library of Sweden. It's just under a metre tall, half a metre wide, and twenty centimetres thick. It weighs slightly more than I do, and its parchment reputedly contains the skins of 160 donkeys. All this shows what can be achieved if you leave everything until the last possible minute and then work like stink.

Shturmovshchina has, for some unjust reason, never made it into an English dictionary, though we do have the equivalent term of a *charette*. Charettes began in Paris in the nineteenth century among students of architecture. Unlike most of the other university disciplines, architects were often made to build little models of the buildings they were designing, using very large pieces of paper. This was a difficult and time-consuming activity, and it also meant that the work was so cumbersome and bulky that it was very hard to hand in.

Consequently, on the day that the work was to be handed in, Parisian architecture students would be forced to hire a cart to transport all their designs and models across Paris to be given to their examiners. Architecture students were not actually so different to their peers in other disciplines, in that they tended to leave their work till the last possible minute. The difference with them was that the last possible minute was spent in a cart, and once a year the would-be Haussmanns could all be seen parading through Paris in their carts still adding little details to their designs and fixing inelegant parts of their models. These were said to be working 'in the cart' or, in French, *en charette*. Somehow the term charette ended up on the other side of the Atlantic with a sense given by the OED of:

> A period of intense (group) work, typically undertaken in order to meet a deadline.

It is somehow comforting to know that whether immured in Bohemia, Soviet Russia, Belle Époque Paris or modern America, everybody procrastinates until the deadline is almost upon them. Even in the Second World War in Britain, with Nazi invasion looming and freedom and civilisation at stake, soldiers would still work in what was known as a *panic party* in an attempt to remedy a week of rest with an hour of intense labour.

Though a panic party was usually a soldiers' shturmovshchina, another military definition is recorded in the *Sydney Sun* (1942):

A route march is an organised shemozzle, while any rush move
is a panic party.

And, just in case you were wondering, this is from *Soldier and
Sailor Words* (1925):

> *Shemozzle*, to, to make off: to get out of the way – e.g., 'We saw
> the M.P.'s (Military Police) coming, so we shemozzled.'

Between your shturmovshchina, charette and panic party, you
should now be as busy as a one-legged tap dancer. You will be
very throng, as they said in rural eighteenth-century England.
Indeed, you may lose all respectability and self-control and
begin to *fisk*, which once meant 'to run about hastily and heed-
lessly'. Fisking is best done with a sheaf of papers in each hand
and a mobile telephone jammed between your head and shoulder. This is also the best time of day to have a heart attack,
should you be so inclined. And even if you aren't, you can liven
up the office by pretending. It would be rather apt, as there's a
lovely little definition in Grose's *Dictionary of the Vulgar Tongue*:

> GRAVE DIGGER: Like a grave digger; up to the a-se in busi-
> ness, and don't know which way to turn.

You may even lose all sense of perspective and forgo your *seven
beller*, which is a naval term for a cup of tea taken exactly half an
hour before the end of a shift. This is on the basis that a watch
in the Royal Navy used to last for four hours, with a bell toll-
ing every thirty minutes. So eight bells signified completion and
seven bells meant near-completion and a cup of tea.

This is also, incidentally, the reason that you can still *beat seven bells* out of somebody in a fistfight. If you were to beat eight bells out of a fellow sailor it would mean that they were dead, that their watch on this watery earth was finally over. But seven bells means Not Quite Dead, or a nice cup of tea, depending on your propensity to violence.

But there is no nice cup of seven bells for he who is *festinating* (that is hurrying) to get everything done before the clock strikes six. In fact, you may be forced to do whatever it is you're doing *frobly*, which is to say indifferently well. If a job is worth doing it is, after all, worth doing badly. There is a splendid journalistic term for this: the *quality of doneness*. This term originated in an editorial meeting of the American magazine *The Weekly Standard* in 2005. The staff were debating whether to use an article that wasn't quite up to snuff or scratch. Everybody felt that it could have been written rather better until the executive editor pointed out its one vital advantage. It might not have the highest quality of writing, but it did have the most important quality of any article: *the quality of doneness.*

If something has the quality of doneness you can forgive its having been done half-arsed or *crawly-mawly* or *frobly-mobly*. It is *upwound, perimplenished, perfurnished, expleted* and ended.

And if it isn't, it can always be put off till tomorrow, which is the precise and technical meaning of the word *pro-* (for) *crastinate* (tomorrow). Indeed, why put off till tomorrow what you can put off till the day after tomorrow? The technical term for this is to *perendinate* a task – a rare word for a common action.

At this late hour you are probably seized with *eleutheromania,* or 'a crazed desire for freedom'. Thomas Carlyle mentioned it in his *History of the French Revolution* but it hasn't been found much since. This is a crying shame, as it can be used in all sorts of situations. You can get out of any dull social event by explaining ruefully to your host that you'd love to stay but just happen to be suffering from a touch of eleutheromania and must be excused. And eleutheromania bites hardest when the working day is nearly done.

So if everything is neatly perendinated, give up and go. But before you leave the office, it may be wise to claim any *estovers* that you may need. Estovers are those parts of your lord's estate to which you, as a faithful serf, are entitled. You may take wood from your lord's forest to repair your cottage, or water from your lord's well, or milk from your lord's fridge, or biros from your lord's stationery cupboard, or loo rolls from your lord's lavatory. Nobody will object, especially if nobody notices. And who would notice a mere *niffle*? A niffle is a Yorkshire term for a trifle or thing of little value. As a verb, *niffling* is the practice of 'not doing very much' or 'stealing a little at a time'. A niffle here and a niffle there and you end up with an awful lot of biros.

This is all nearly legal and utterly natural. Biologists even have a word for it: *lestobiosis*, which comes from the Greek *lestos* meaning 'robber', and *biosis* meaning 'way of life'. It's defined in the OED as:

> A form of symbiosis found among certain social insects in which a small species inhabits the nest of a larger one and feeds on the food stored there, or on the brood of the larger species.

And it would seem remarkably unfair to deny office workers a privilege that is accorded to the humble ant. So grab a good handful of biros and maybe a couple of chairs and head for the *vomitoria*.

A vomitorium is *not* a room in which ancient Romans would throw up halfway through a banquet in order to make room for the next course. That's a myth. A vomitorium is simply a passage by which you can exit a building, usually a theatre. But the word can happily be applied to any building, and it is rather poetic and lovely to imagine all these personified office blocks puking their merry workers out into the evening air.

Chapter 13

6 p.m. – After Work

Strolling around – arranging your evening

❧

It is the violet hour, the crepuscular, twilit hour when (on average) the sun drops into the western bay and night comes. If you are reading this in midsummer in the Arctic Circle, my apologies – I can deal only in averages.

It is, as I was saying, *cockshut*, the 'close of evening at which poultry go to roost'. The sky *obnubilates* (or darkens) and all sorts of words beginning with *vesper-* come out to play in the twilight.

When the planet Venus shines at dusk, it becomes Hesperus, the evening star. And if you pronounce the H as a V you get the evening service of the church: *vespers*. From that you get *vespertine* (belonging to the evening), *advesperate* ('to wax night'), *vesperal* (a song to be sung in the evening), and *vespertilionize* (to convert into a bat). I'm not sure if that last word is truly useful for those who aren't of the vampiric persuasion; but, for those that are, it is invaluable.

The best vesper word, though, is *vespery*. Vesperies were the exercises and disputations practised in the evening by scholars at the Sorbonne University in Paris. The word made it into a couple of English dictionaries back in the seventeenth century but has since pretty much vanished. This is a shame, as it's a splendid catch-all term for whatever it is that you do after work. Your vesperies might consist of a visit to a gym (if you are *exergastic* or 'tending to work out'), a supply run into a supermarket, or a stroll or a sprint to the nearest bar. All are vesperies, and each person chooses their own.

If you do go to the gym, you are liable to be *tread-wheeled*, which is, according to the OED, a transitive verb meaning 'to inflict the discipline of the treadmill upon'. This refers, of course, to the use of treadmills as a punishment in Victorian prisons. This was viewed, even at the time, as a barbaric practice[1] and was abolished in 1898. It was then slyly reintroduced in the twentieth century for those who wanted to experience the misery of a nineteenth-century prison without the necessity of committing any crime.

Over in nineteenth-century France, they had a much better idea for how to pass this twilit hour: *flânerie*.

Flânerie

Flânerie is often cited as one of those French words for which there can never be a true English translation. People harp on about how neither strolling nor loitering nor lingering nor promenading can ever express what flânerie really is. Such

---

[1] I refer any defenders of gym-culture to a plea for prison reform written in 1824: 'The labour of the tread-mill is irksome, dull, monotonous, and disgusting to the last degree. A man does not see his work, does not know what he is doing, what progress he is making; there is no room for art, contrivance, ingenuity and superior skill – all which are the cheering circumstances of human labour.'

people cannot have checked the OED, as they would have noticed that we don't need to translate the word: we have simply nicked it, along with the related verb *flâner* and the noun *flâneur*, one who indulges in flânerie.

Even though the word has been kidnapped by English, it is still very hard to define exactly what it is. The OED does a reasonable job with 'A lounger or saunterer, an idle "man about town"'. But this doesn't get to the true essence of the business, for which we will have to turn, reluctantly, to the French.

Put simply, the flâneur is the average French citizen raised to the level of a spiritual ideal. They wander about talking to nobody and doing very little. You can see what the OED is getting at, but it's so much more than that. The concept was promulgated best by Charles Baudelaire:

> The crowd is his domain, as air is that of a bird, or water that of a fish. His passion and his profession, it's to become one with the crowd. For the perfect flâneur, for the ideal idler, for the impassioned observer, it is a vast joy to be at home among the passers-by, in the swirl of people, in the movement, in the fugitive and the infinite. To be away from his home, but to be at home everywhere; to see the world, to be at the centre of the world, but to be concealed from the world; such are the smaller pleasures of these independent, impassioned and impartial souls, which language can only clumsily define.

Flânerie is an idea that was expanded and refined through the nineteenth and early twentieth century. It is the practice of sitting alone in a café observing the world hurrying past and trying to read a life in each face. It is the practice of wandering through narrow streets and seeing people on their balconies or children hurrying home from school. It is the practice of smoking endless moody cigarettes as you *scamander* through the city.

Scamander, by the way, is the sister verb of *meander*. The river Maeander winds, by a preposterously curly-whirly route, through Izmir in Turkey. The ancient Greeks were very taken with the twistings of the Maeander, and their chief geographer, a fellow called Strabo, declared that 'its course is so exceedingly winding that anything winding is called a meander'. Of course he declared that in Greek, but the term was nonetheless carried over into English, so that we moderns may meander around as much as we like. If you feel that the Maeander isn't the river for you, you may pick the Scamander, another Turkish watercourse now known as the Karamenderes. The Scamander wound mazily across the windy plain before the walls of Troy, and is where Achilles did some of his best killing.[2] The Scamander made a brief go of ousting its fellow river, and a dictionary of the street slang of Victorian London defines scamander as:

To wander about without a settled purpose.

There is, though, no need for the terms to fight. They rhyme so well that one can happily meander and scamander in the same sentence. By a process of alliteration we may add in here the *scoperloit*, an old north-country word for 'the time of idleness' when weary labourers would lounge around beneath a vespertine tree, which they would have called the *mogshade*. They might even, in their rustic way, have indulged in a spot of

---

[2] Just after his paranormal breakfast described in Chapter 3.

sauntry, which is the act of sauntering, and perhaps the closest native equivalent to flânerie.

Evening arrangements

As the *dimpsy murkens* and the sky obnubilates into night's blackness it is time to sort out exactly what you are going to do with yourself this evening. You may, of course, settle down to watch the gogglebox for the rest of the night. I can't stop you, but if you do, I fear that there are few arcane medieval words to help you in your glaze-eyed channel hopping. So instead, I shall blithely assume that you will spend the evening out on the town with your friends. Should you stay in, this reference work will cease to function.

However, trying to arrange a good evening's *compotation* and *commensation* is always a tricky task. All societies are *commensal*, to some extent or another, which is the anthropologist's term for the rules of who you can and cannot sit down to dinner with. In the ancient Near East commensality was considered immensely important, to the extent that if you sat down to have a nice supper with a sinner, that made you a sinner too. It is this strict principle of commensality (from *com* meaning 'with' and *mensa* meaning 'table') that makes Jesus's sitting down with the wine-bibbers and tax collectors such a prickly point in the gospels. A man could be judged by the company he kept at table.

Even the Messiah, trying to arrange a nice jolly before he got riveted to a plank, had to go through all sorts of weird shenanigans just to get a table:

And he sent Peter and John, saying, Go and prepare us the passover, that we may eat. And they said unto him, Where wilt thou that we prepare? And he said unto them, Behold, when ye are entered into the city, there shall a man meet you, bearing a pitcher of water; follow him into the house where he entereth in. And ye shall say unto the goodman of the house, The Master saith unto thee, Where is the guestchamber, where I shall eat the passover with my disciples? And he shall shew you a large upper room furnished: there make ready.

Jesus also had the tricky task of picking the guests for his farewell bash, and he seems to have managed eleven chums and one stinker. There always seems to be what a British soldier of the Second World War out on leave would call a *constable*:

The Constable. Unwanted person who attaches himself to another; a hanger-on who refuses to take the hint.

American servicemen had their own equivalent rank to constable, described in the same dictionary of Second World War slang:

Heel. This is an Americanism for a hanger-on, and in the service it means a fellow who seeks your company for the sake of a free drink. Thus HEELING, paying a heel for something.

Constable seems to me a much more useful word, as it can be used without the person in question having any idea of what you mean. 'Hello, Constable', you can say with an amicable smile, and they may even assume that the word is a mark of respect. You can go further and explain to the others that so-and-so is the Constable for the evening. Thus everybody can be set to leap out of the window and hare off down the street the moment their back is turned. Judas Iscariot, however, was definitely a *heel*.

The question of how to avoid unwanted friends is one that has been bothering English-speakers for centuries. At Cambridge University in the late eighteenth century they had four distinct ways of not bumping into an old chum on the street:

> TO CUT: (Cambridge.) To renounce acquaintance with any one is to cut him. There are several species of the cut. Such as the cut direct, the cut indirect, the cut sublime, the cut infernal, &c.

> The CUT DIRECT, is to start across the street, at the approach of the obnoxious person in order to avoid him.

> The CUT INDIRECT, is to look another way, and pass without appearing to observe him.

> The CUT SUBLIME, is to admire the top of King's College Chapel, or the beauty of the passing clouds, till he is out of sight.

> The CUT INFERNAL, is to analyze the arrangement of your shoe-strings, for the same purpose.

The cut infernal is the most effective, and, while you're down there, do you see the little plastic bits on the ends of your shoe-laces? They're called *aglets*. Jesus, I suppose, would have had to practise the cut sublime. How different theological history would have been if, in the Garden of Gethsemane, when Judas came to *judasly* (yes, that's a real word) kiss Him, Jesus had simply pretended not to notice and just stared up at the Temple Mount.

He could also have been helped by two little-known negatives. To recognise a chap is to know (*cognise*) him again (*re*). However, if you cease to recognise a fellow you *decognise* him. This is, to be fair, a rare word, and so far as I can tell it has only ever been used in a parliamentary debate about the position of Charles II,[3] but it is still useful in phrases such as: 'I'm so sorry, old chap, I must have decognised you.' You can even formalise things by sending somebody you really don't like a *devitation*, an obsolete and rare word that is the exact opposite of an invitation. So maybe a nice formal thing written on card with your name in curly letters at the top requesting the pleasure of _____'s absence.

Some people just keep popping up and clapping you on the shoulder when your shoulder least needs to be clapped (incidentally, a *shoulderclapper* is a term for somebody who is unnecessarily friendly). Old acquaintances you thought consigned to the dustbin of your address book sometimes appear with an almost rasputinish obstinacy. Such people are known as *didappers*. A didapper was, originally, a name for the Little Grebe or *Podiceps minor*, a kind of water bird that dives for its food and, just when you think that it must have been eaten by a pike, pops up again on the other side of the pond looking sleek and well fed. The English libertine Charles Colton, in the same book in which he coined the phrase 'Imitation is the sincerest form of

---

[3] Not in a Nell Gwynn way.

flattery', wrote of John Wilkes that:

> There are some men who are fortune's favourites, and who,
> like cats, light for ever up their legs; Wilkes was one of those
> didappers, whom, if you had stripped naked, and thrown over
> Westminster bridge, you might have met on the very next day,
> with a bag-wig on his head, a sword by his side, a laced coat
> upon his back, and money in his pocket.

But even as you try to dodge heels and constables and are busy
hurling shoulderclapping didappers naked from Westminster
Bridge, other people are attempting to do the same to you.

What about your friends, your *makes*, *marrows*, *sociuses*,
sociates, *compadres*, *consociators*, *belamies* (from the French *bel
ami*, beautiful friend), *friars*, *familiars*, *inwards* and *tillicums*?
You may send out your invitations by text and telephone, but
they may remain mere *pollicitations* – an offer made but not
yet accepted – while your so-called friends wait around for a
slightly better prospect. Damn those tillicums (*tillicum* or *tili-
kum* is, by the way, the Chinook word for people, which then
came to mean a member of the same tribe, and then got taken
up by English-speakers to mean chum).

Rather than being picky about it, it may be time to run back
after all those didappers and constables and hoist the *gin pennant*. The gin pennant is a real flag used by the British Navy to
invite people round for a drink. It is first recorded (or at least
remembered) in the 1940s as a small green triangular pennant
with a white wine glass in the middle. If it is hoisted then the
officers of any accompanying ships are invited on board for
drinks. However, it is very, very small.

You see, the officers of the Royal Navy were attempting, as the old phrase goes, to *have their mense and their meat*. 'Mense' means politeness and 'meat' meant food, so trying to have your mense and your meat was trying to earn a reputation for hospitality without actually giving any food away. So this tiny gin pennant is hoisted very quietly at sunset in the hope that nobody will notice. But it must be hoisted occasionally, just so you can say that you did, and didn't you see it? What a shame! We were so hoping to give you our whole allowance of rum.

In fact, several traditions have arisen concerning the gin pennant, which these days is green at each end with a white centre and green glass upon it. You can, for example, when aboard somebody else's ship, attempt to hoist their gin pennant and thus force them to give you free booze. However, if you are caught doing this then you have to invite them back to your ship for the same. Gin pennants can even be flown privately above the bar, just to show those already present that the drinks are on you for the evening. It therefore seems to me that the Royal Navy has a splendid piece of English ready to be taken up by us landlubbers, as in: 'I had nothing whatever to do, so I just hoisted the gin pennant, phoned everyone, and had a splendid evening.'

But before hoisting your gin pennant, you should make sure that you actually have some gin worth flagging up. You'll probably need tonic and lemons and perhaps even some food as well. And for all those you will need not just a market, but a supermarket.

Chapter 14

7 p.m. – Shopping

Disorientation – ecstasy in the supermarket

❦

Gruen transfer

It is about time that you popped to the shops. Man cannot live on bread alone, but it's a good start. Sadly, these days, none but the most fastidious potter from little shop to little shop buying their beef at a butcher, their bread at a baker and their *costards* (large apples) from a costermonger. No. Our markets must be super or even hyper: cloud-capped palaces of commerce. Places that quite deliberately blow your mind even as you walk in the door in a process called the *Gruen transfer*.

Victor Gruen was born Victor Greenbaum in Austria in 1903. In 1938 he fled the Nazis and arrived in America with 'an architect's degree, eight dollars and no English'. It was with the first of those that he created something wonderful: the modern shopping mall. Gruen is the acknowledged originator and master of the mall, as he designed over fifty of them in the USA and accidentally gave his name to the strange mental effect they have on you.

Shopping malls rarely have any windows on the outside. There is a good reason for this: if you could see the world beyond the window you would be able to orientate yourself and might not get lost. Shopping malls have maps that are unreadable even to the most skilled cartographer. There is a good reason for this: if you could read the map you would be able to find your way to the shop you meant to go to without getting lost. Shopping malls look rather the same whichever way you turn. There is a reason for this too: shopping malls are built to disorientate you, to spin you around, to free you from the original petty purpose for which you came and make you wander like Cain past rows and rows of shops thinking to yourself, 'Ooh! I should actually go in there and get something. Might as well, seeing as I'm here.' And this strange mental process, this freeing of the mind from all sense of purpose or reason, is known to retail analysts as the Gruen transfer.

The term Gruen transfer does not seem to have appeared until a decade after Victor Gruen's death in 1980, but it is now an essential part of planning a shop. It is the combination of sensory overload and spatial amazement that means you buy many more things than you meant to and thus keep the whole place profitable. It is what turns you from *traffic* – the people passing a shop – to *footfall* – the people entering the shop. And, oh, what linguistic beauties are within!

The ecstasy of the supermarket

To the uninitiated, supermarkets can seem rather boring places; places, indeed, that you just go to buy things in. But to the initiated they are palaces of poetry.

For starters, do you see those lines of free-standing, two-sided shelves that divide the aisles? They are not called free-standing, two-sided shelves, because that would be much too dull for the race of poets that manage supermarkets. They are called *gondolas*, because to the romantic mind of the retail manager they resemble nothing so much as a Venetian punt.

This marine motif is taken up with the standalone displays, the little tubs of crisps or tights or whatever is on offer, which are called *islands*, lapped by waves of customers like a consumer ocean. And look up! Those strings and bars suspended from the ceiling are the *aisle-leapers*, strange sure-footed godlings who jump above us, laughing at the mortals below. And their role in the great mythology is to support the *danglers* – the pennants that advertise Twenty, Thirty and Forty Percent Off Selected Products! If the danglers are made of such a material that they may sway in the soft zephyrs of the air-conditioning they are *wobblers*, which are thus the supermercantile equivalent of cherubim.

Nothing is too fantastical for the inherently magical mind of the retail manager. The *Light Thief*, a creature never imagined by the Brothers Grimm, is their name for a display that has no illumination of its own but, painted in merry fluorescent colours and bejewelled with reflective surfaces, steals the light of others and shines itself. In traditional supermarket folklore the Light Thief is the eternal enemy of the *Shelf Miser*, that little tray affixed to the side of the gondola that sticks out a bit into the aisle and thus contains more goods than tradition or equality would allow.

The Shelf Miser beetles o'er the *price channel*, the thin strip where the costs of items and their Every Day Low Price are shown, and casts his niggardly shadow upon the *kick band*, that little strip a few inches high at the base of the gondola that is darkly coloured so as not to show the marks of scuffing shoes or the drips from an unruly mop.

There is high and low. Those cardboard thingies around the top of a bottle? They're *bottle glorifiers*. Those hard plastic packs that contain the product in a little bubble and are absolutely impossible to open? They're *blister packs*.

Nothing in the supermarket is what it seems to the dreary crowds who know not its glories. They pass by discounts that are for a limited period only, without realising that they are standing next to an *exploding offer*. Where two products compete for shelf-space, or *facing* as it is anthropomorphically called, they fight to the death. And if those two products are manufactured by the same parent company, this fight is known to bloodthirsty retail outlets as *cannibalism*. So when Coca-Cola competes with Sprite, Magnum with Cornetto, or Tampax with Always Ultra, the retail manager sees brother eating the body of brother. No mere Venetian gondola, idle up its sleepy canal, ever held such scenes of anthropophagy, where sibling devours the flesh of sibling while the offers detonate below.

And at the checkout you suddenly find love. For when you are given a store-card or collect points towards a future purchase this is known as *romancing the customer*. Of course, the romance is really just someone making calculations and offering you what they can afford to give in exchange for your favours, but all romance is like that really, and it's best to go along with it.

With fluttering heart, it's little wonder the impulse buys you whimsically commit to at the point of sale! For humankind cannot bear very much supermarket. It is too grand and too terrible, too tempting and too fantastical. When you are on the street again and looking around at this blank world, you will know that it can never match the dreams and nightmares that lie beyond the Gruen transfer. When Faustus asks Mephistopheles how he has escaped from Hell, the fallen angel replies:

> Why, this is Hell, nor am I out of it.
> Think'st thou that I, who saw the face of God
> And tasted the eternal joys of Heaven,
> Am not tormented with ten thousand hells
> In being deprived of everlasting bliss?

And so it is with supermarkets. Be not afraid. You will return, if only for the romance. But for now, it is time for supper.

Chapter 15

8 p.m. – Supper

*Dietary requirements – seating arrangements
– making conversation – avoiding conversation
– hogging the wine – finishing supper – avoiding the bill*

⌒⌒⌒

It is time to sidle *supperward* (a pleasant little word that gets its own entry in the dictionary), although before we do, we ought to sort out the difference between *supper* and *dinner*. Supper is, according to the OED, the last meal of the day. (It goes on to contradict itself by mentioning a *rere supper*, which is a second supper consumed after the main supper; but we'll let that pass.) Dinner is the main meal of the day. Supper can therefore sometimes be dinner, and dinner can sometimes be supper. It all depends on the size of your lunch, or indeed breakfast. It's such a thorny question that the OED makes a rare venture into sociology for *dinner*'s definition:

> The chief meal of the day, eaten originally, and still by the majority of people, about the middle of the day (cf. German *Mittagessen*), but now, by the professional and fashionable classes, usually in the evening.

So assuming that you are professional or fashionable, and perhaps both at once, we shall hereinafter refer to this meal as supper, except when we don't.

Another useful word here is *tocsin*, meaning a bell rung as an alarm, but only because you need it to understand Lord Byron's supperish lines:

> That all-softening, overpowering knell,
> The tocsin of the soul, the dinner bell.

This is an example of *coenaculous*, or supper-loving, poetry. Coenaculous (deriving from the Latin *cenaculum* (meaning dining room) but somehow obtaining an unnecessary O) is a curiously obscure word, when you consider that man is a uniformly coenaculous creature. Indeed, the rest of the day can often seem like a long preprandial tease. As Sir Francis Bacon said: 'Hope is a good breakfast, but it is a bad supper.'

Once the dinner bell has sounded and the guests are gathered, whether at a restaurant or at home, the first thing to do is to try to work out whether this is a *Dutch feast*, 'where the entertainer gets drunk before his guest'. Having established that your host is, indeed, *bumpsy*, you can get on with the usual chit-chat and introducing yourself to people who remember you.

At this point, there's usually a panic as it turns out that one person is a vegetarian, another kosher, another is halal and a fourth wants to check that the ingredients were all humanely and sustainably sourced. At this point you can apologetically admit to being a *halalcor*. You can even try making a big fuss about it, provided, that is, that nobody looks in the OED and discovers:

Halalcor One of the lowest and most despised class in India, Iran, etc., (lit.) to whom everything is lawful food.

If caught out like this, you should simply change tack and insist that you *only* eat food that is inhumanely and unsustainably sourced, as it tastes better. Anything for a little trouble.

Once everybody's dietary foibles have been established, along with the host's drunkenness, everybody can sit down and prepare to eat.

Marshalling

People are *marshalled* to their places at the supper table. This meaning of the verb predates the 'marshalling-your-troops' sense by seventy years. Mind you, before that it meant to look after horses, which shows how much respect people had for their dinner guests in the fifteenth century.

The place that you shall be marshalled to is the *cenacle*, the proper word for the chamber in which supper is to be taken (from the same Latin root as coenaculous above). Indeed, the word cenacle originally referred only to the mysterious room in which the Last Supper was taken by Jesus and co-dinnerists. Once in the cenacle, Jesus encountered the same problem that faces any supperist, namely where to sit everybody. He had had this problem before; in Matthew Chapter 20:

Then came to him the mother of Zebedee's children with her sons, worshipping him, and desiring a certain thing of him. And he said unto her, What wilt thou? She saith unto him, Grant

that these my two sons may sit, the one on thy right hand, and
the other on the left, in thy kingdom. But Jesus answered and
said, Ye know not what ye ask.

This sort of thing can indeed be tiresome and it's probably why
he ended up at the Last Supper with one chap's head on his lap
and another annoyingly trying to dip bread at exactly the same
time. Nor are those of us with lesser parentage exempted from
these tribulations. Who shall sit where? Who, as they would say
in medieval times, should *begin the board* and take precedence
at table?

Technically, the host of the meal should *hold the dais*, but
as we've established that they're drunk, it's time to sit *at one's
reward*, or in a much better place at table than you deserve.

It would have been much easier in Roman times when everybody *discumbed*, which is to say that they ate lying down on a
triclinum that ran around three sides of the table. That meant
that if two people particularly wanted the same place they could
just lie on top of each other. However, discumbency may cause
indigestion. So it is best to merely grab your seat and *lollop* or
'lean with one's elbows on the table'.

Making conversation

Seventeen centuries ago, a chap called Athenaeus of Naucratis
wrote a book about the perfect conversation over supper. The
ideal subjects for conversation were, according to Athenaeus,
absolutely bloody everything, with a particular focus on homo-
sexuality and lexicography.

Neither of these subjects need detain us (except perhaps to note that the 'Celts, although they have very beautiful women, prefer boys'), for what concerns us here is not the content of the book, but the title. Athenaeus called his book the *Deipnosophistae*, which means, literally, the 'kitchen-wisemen' but is more usually translated as those who talk wisely over supper. From this we get the English word *deipnosophist*, first recorded in 1581, which means 'a chap who talks wisely at supper' or alternatively 'a master of the art of dining'.

The Greek word *deipnon* has given English a couple of other interesting little words: *deipno-diplomatic*, which means 'of or pertaining to dining and diplomacy', and *deipnophobia*, which is a 'dread of dinner parties', an emotion more often felt than named. But both those words have been used only once, whereas deipnosophism has survived and endured as a recondite yet necessary art. Only a true master of deipnosophism can tell the difference between a *colloquist*, one who takes part in a conversation, and a *colloquialist*, one who excels in conversation.

For my own part, knowing that I lack the qualifications to speak wisely, I have instead learned to excel at the art of *rhubarbing*, which is the last refuge of the failed deipnosophist. To rhubarb is to say the word 'rhubarb' over and over again in a low, indistinct voice. The reason that this strange verb has made the dictionary is that rhubarb is the standard word that actors use in a crowd scene when they wish to mimic the sound of general conversation. So when Mark Antony comes out on stage all the actors are rhubarbing, and when he shouts 'Friends, Romans, countrymen, lend me your ears', they cease to rhubarb.

Nobody knows why rhubarb was picked for this purpose, or

exactly when, but it's etymologically perfect. 'Rhubarb' comes from the ancient Greek *Rha Barbaron*, which literally means 'foreign rhubarb', because rhubarb was a strange oriental delicacy imported to the classical world via Russia from Tibet. 'Barbaron' was Greek for foreigner because foreigners were all *barbarians*. But the important thing was that the barbarians were called barbarians because they spoke a foreign and unintelligible language, which sounded to the Greeks as though they were just saying 'bar-bar-bar-bar' all the time (roughly in the way that we say 'blah-blah-blah' or 'yadda-yadda-yadda'). Therefore, the ancient word for unintelligible mumbling has, after a journey of several thousand years, come straight back to its original purpose.

Rhubarbing is particularly useful if you want to disguise the fact that nobody wants to talk to you, although you must remember not to use it when the waiter comes to take your order.

Avoiding conversation

Society is now one polished horde
Formed of two mighty tribes, the bores and bored.

Lord Byron

Better to be a rhubarber than a *bromide*. Bromide used to be used as a sedative and was therefore taken up as a nineteenth-century American term for a fellow who can put you to sleep, with the efficiency of good Valium, merely by talking. A dedicated bromide moves through his subject with the same tortoise-speed as a drill boring its way through granite, hence the more usual term: a bore.[1]

However, in this I feel (as an inveterate and ambitious bore myself) that bromide is not quite the right word. Boredom is not merely the lack of stimulation, it is an active property. Sit somebody in an empty room or in front of the proverbial drying paint and they will be quite content for a while, musing on something or another, and, provided that they are over the age of ten, restlessness may not set in for quite a while. But a Class-A bore can have you frantic within seconds. I personally have merely to say the words, 'Ah, I'm glad you asked me that ...' to observe a terrified, hunted light come into my interlocutor's/victim's eyes. The only way to stop me is immediate *kittle pitchering*, which is amply described in a late eighteenth-century dictionary.

> KITTLE PITCHERING. A jocular method of hobbling or bothering a troublesome teller of long stories: this is done by contradicting some very immaterial circumstance at the beginning of the narration, the objections to which being settled, others are immediately started to some new particular of like consequence; thus impeding, or rather not suffering him to enter into, the main story. Kittle pitchering is often practiced in confederacy, one relieving the other, by which the design is rendered less obvious.

Why is it called kittle pitchering? Ah, I'm glad you asked me that. Well, *kittle* is an old word for tickling, and a *pitcher* is somebody who loads hay onto a cart, and hay, being dry, is proverbially

---

[1] The French *bourre*, meaning padding, may also be responsible. I could go on.

boring (Thomas Gray once commented that trying to read Aristotle was like eating dried hay).

And what do you call the rhetorical act of asking a question and then answering it yourself? Ah, I'm glad you asked me that. It is called *anthypophora*, and was a practice much beloved of the ancient Greeks. And what do you call it when you keep doing this again and again and again? That's *dianoea*. And why do I keep using these tiresome techniques? Quite simply because it disguises the fact that nobody is interested and that nobody can get a word in edgewise anyhow.

In fact, once I've got a good rhythm going with my dianoea, the only thing to do is to attack directly by interrupting. However, it is of no use simply asking, 'May I interrupt?', as such polite proposals are rarely accepted. The best thing to do in this situation is to use a particularly obscure and puerile synonym of the word 'interrupt'. So lean forward, look the speaker in the eyes, and say in a deep and loud voice: 'I would like to *interjaculate*.'

A long silence may be left after the use of this phrase before asking somebody to pass the salt. The Latin *jaculari* only means 'throw', so interjaculate means 'throw in between'. Put an E on the front and you have throw out. There's even a related word *interjaculatory*, which is defined as 'expressed in parenthetical ejaculations'. For example, a writer in *Blackwood's Magazine* in 1827 mentions how the arrival of the host's child 'smites a large dinner-party mute, or into interjaculatory admiration of its hereditary beauties'.

Thus can the monologue be turned to a *duologue*, and thence to a *tetralogue* (there is, for some reason, no English word for a conversation between three people), and hence into a free-for-all *collocation*.

Who skinks?

With the conversation resting in an uneasy truce, it is possible to get down to matters truly *cenatory* (or 'related to supper') such as eating and drinking. The first thing to ask is 'Who *skinks*?', which is an old-fashioned way of asking who the hell is meant to be pouring out the drinks.

Often, though, there is no designated skinker and the bottle is simply wandering around the table. It will usually be seen cowering at the far end and out of reach, which means that you'll have to get somebody to pass it along – clockwise.

In our modern, fallen age the practice of passing things clockwise around the table is confined to only the poshest and most hidebound of dinners, and even there only to the port and snuff, but it was once universal. Everything had to be done in the direction of the sun.

If you spend a whole day standing still and staring southward you will see the sun rise upon your left and then trot across the sky in front of you before setting to the right. If you stand facing northward all day you will see the shadow of your head doing the same thing on the other side, making you the living *gnomon* of a sundial.

You will only face south, though, if you're in the northern hemisphere, where the sun spends most of its time more or less slightly south of you. Botswanans, New Zealanders and other occupants of the southern hemisphere will look north for the sun. (I must refer Equitorialists to previous comments about the average.) Clocks were built to imitate sundials in the northern hemisphere, and that is why clockwise is sunwise. If clocks had been invented in Australia, they would go the other way.

Once upon a time it was considered right and proper to do everything in the direction of the sun, i.e. clockwise. If you were, for example, to walk around a church, you would do so sunwise. If a group of peasants were passing around their lunchtime loaf of bread, they would do so sunwise, since to pass the other way would be terribly bad luck – this is called doing something *withershins*. In fact, a standard way for a witch to curse you was to walk nine times about your house withershins; and when witches danced in a circle, they did (and do) so withershins. Everything good had to be done clockwise.

This sensible precaution against the Arch-Fiend did have some drawbacks. You could find yourself in a seventeenth-century tavern gazing longingly at a bottle but unable to reach for it. So all sorts of phrases were invented to hint to whoever had the bottle that they should get a bloody move on. 'Remember Parson Malham', 'Who is Peter Lug?', 'Who has any lands in Appleby?' were all cries that would come from the droughty end of the table. All of these phrases are, so far as anyone can tell, completely meaningless.[2]

Today, the belief that doing anything withershins is bad luck is confined to the high table of Oxbridge colleges, where they know that it's all true. And the current standard phrase to get the bottle moving is: 'Do you know the Bishop of Norwich?'

However, it is vital to remember that, technically, the port should always be passed to the right if you are in the southern hemisphere.

---

[2] Although there is something odd that I noticed. Do you remember the mysterious Sir Posthumus Hoby in Chapter 3? No? Oh well. He was MP for Appleby and, as a Puritan, would probably be against drinking. Peter Lug was also a name for someone who hogs the bottle.

Finishing off

A fine strategic brain is required when passing the wine around, as you must try to predict who will be left with the *swank*, a dialect word recorded in an early eighteenth-century dictionary:

> Swank [at Bocking in Essex] that remainder of liquor at the bottom of a tankard, pot or cup, which is just sufficient for one draught; which is not accounted good manners to divide with the left hand man, and according to the quantity is called either a large or little swank.[3]

If you have managed to obtain the swank, guzzle it down as fast as you can and explain about Essex later. If somebody else has it, then you may suggest that you do the decent Victorian thing and *buz*, which is:

> To share equally the last of a bottle of wine, when there is not enough for a full glass for each of the party.

But what of the food? As the dinner draws to a close it is vital, in the interests of good manners, that you remember to leave a *tailor's mense*. In the days when a tailor came to fit you in your own home, it was customary to provide him with a light meal. This he would eat lightly. If he finished it all off, you would be left with the awkward feeling that perhaps you hadn't provided

---

[3] A hundred years later the term was still going, although this time it had moved across the county to Braintree where, in 1813, 'A pint of beer is divided into three parts or draughts; the first is called Neckum, the second Sinkum, and the third Swank or Swankum'.

enough food for the poor tradesman. To pre-empt such worries the tailor would always nearly finish his meal but leave a little bit on the side of the plate to show that he was stuffed and couldn't possibly eat another bite if his life depended upon it. As we've seen, mense was another word for tact or politeness, so this tactful gobbet of food was called a tailor's mense. Thus:

> *Tailor's mense*, the morsel of meat which a country tailor leaves at dinner, when working out, that he may not be charged with indecently eating all up.

In the late nineteenth century, people got very precise as to exactly how much you should leave as a tailor's mense. One book of 1872 specifies that:

> A 'tailor's mense,' ration, or allowance, is, according to an old saying, a small portion of a meal left for good manners, only one-ninth part of the quantity required for a man.

The recommended daily food intake for a man is usually 2,500 calories, and so dividing that up into three equal meals a day, we can conclude that a tailor's mense is 93.6 calories, which is about the same as one large fried egg.

Even with a fried egg gleaming on the side of your plate, though, you may for reasons purely of comfort adjust your belt to the most expansive setting. This is called the *yule hole*, and is meant to be used only after Christmas dinner. However, in *A Complete Collection of Scottish Proverbs Explained and Made Intelligible to the English Reader* (1818) the author notes that telling your host that you have 'Set the bag to the old stent [stretch], and the belt to the yule hole' is terribly polite as it implies that 'we eat as heartily as we did at Christmas'.

If, though, you are only using the yule hole out of politeness, it's a good thing to remember this before standing up.

Thanking your host

Now all that remains (aside from the tailor's mense) is the duty of thanking whoever has *bedinnered* you, bedinnering being providing with dinner. Obviously, this should only be done if you actually thought that the supper was up to snuff. If it wasn't, you could say 'Thank you for that collation', and it would only be much later, when your host was flicking through Dr Johnson's dictionary, that they would find that you meant it was 'a treat less than a feast'.

My own standard phrase here is to say that I have been *golopshusly* (or deliciously) bedinnered, before calmly handing over the bill. This has the desired effect on all but the most impudent, in which case you must simply agree to having a *blind man's dinner*, which is one where you run away without paying. If your supper has been taken in a private dwelling then the same thing applies to the washing up. Simply explain that you are awfully sorry but you cannot stay a moment longer as you see by your watch that it is *quafftide*.

Chapter 16

9 p.m. – Drinking

*Persuading others to – choosing a bar
– opening the door – approaching the bar – ordering
– drinking – the results of drinking – empties
– forms of drunkenness*

ᢙᢍᢓ

Picking your ale-knights

You are fed, but you are not yet sufficiently watered, and man cannot live on supper alone. Indeed, the main purpose of supper is to make sure that you are not subjecting your body to the indignity of *dry-drinking*, which is to say, in a seventeenth-century way, boozing on an empty stomach.

However, there are various tasks that must be performed before you can declare with confidence that it is *quafftide*, which is a lovely old term meaning the time of drinking (rather like eventide or morningtide, but a lot more damaging to the liver). First, you will have to explain to your co-supperists that they want a drink too. A lot of people are strangely ignorant of the fact that they are yearning to stay up all night deliberately impairing their mental faculties. However, you must get them along, as if you drink alone it is much harder to avoid buying your round.

A few people will concede immediately that they are up for a *small go*. The definition of this phrase (in a dictionary of Second World War services slang) is not very promising:

> **A Small go.** A reasonable night out with everybody happy and nobody drunk.

But a small go is easily enlarged, and can be considered the Trojan Horse of an evening's entertainment. A little *compotation* (drinking together) can open the gates for a *perpotation* ('the act of drinking largely' according to Dr Johnson). So to those who insist on a small go, you can insist that that was what you had in mind yourself, and you were only planning to have one little tipple. Such little lies, or *taradiddles* as they used to be called, are merely truths that aren't yet true.

However, there may be others who insist that they don't want a drink at all. With these people there is no gentle cajoling to be done; all you can do is hurl insults at them. 'You *drink-water!*' you can shout. '*Nephalist! Hydropot! Wowser!*' All that these words really mean is teetotaller, but hydropot, even though it's only Latin for 'water drinker', has a lovely ring to it; and only the Australians could have come up with wowser, which the OED defines as 'a fanatical or determined opponent of intoxicating drink'.

It is the old war between the *antithalians* and the *apolaustics*, and everybody has to pick which side they're on right now. Thalia is the Muse of Comedy, the Grace of Plenty and the ancient deity of good fun. If you are against her, you are antithalian, a word that, admittedly, has only one documented use in 1818. On the other side are the apolaustics, from the Greek *apolaustikos* meaning enjoyment. The war between these two armies is the eternal conflict of humanity. The antithalians are better organised, but the apolaustics have all the camp followers.

At this point the obstinately funless will probably just scamper home. Good riddance. All that are left are *owlers*.

Owler One who goes abroad at night, like an owl.

Choosing a drunkery

Anyone who thinks a bar is a bar is a bar has not read enough dictionaries. There are myriad distinctive subtleties to be observed. For example, Dr Johnson, who occasionally interrupted his lexicography with night-long boozing-bouts, insisted:

> **Alehouse**. n.s. [Sax. ealhus.] A house where ale is publickly sold; a tipling house. It is distinguished from a tavern where they sell wine.

Each drink has its proper purveyor. There are whisky-houses, rum-holes, gin-joints or occasionally -palaces, wine-lodges, punch-houses, and beer-halls, -gardens, -cellars, -parlours and, inevitably, -bellies.

You must choose your *potation-shop* wisely, for not all *sluiceries* are equal. For example, you might be tempted to visit a *speakeasy blind tiger* (if you were in nineteenth-century USA). A newspaper of 1857 records:

> I sees a kinder pigeon-hole cut in the side of a house, and over
> the hole, in big writin', 'Blind Tiger, ten cents a sight.' ... That
> 'blind tiger' was an arrangement to evade the law, which won't
> let 'em sell licker there, except by the gallon.

And as a gallon is really pushing it for what was meant to be a small do, a blind tiger (or *blind pig*, as they were also called) would be a bit much. Inexperienced drinkers should instead attend a *fuddling-school*, where the fine arts and crafts of fuddling may be explained to them by a competent teacher.

Fuddling is a recondite verb that lies behind the common adjective *befuddled*, which technically means drunk. Fuddling is drinking. Nobody knows quite where the word comes from. It is not, alas, a frequentative, as *sparkle* is of *spark* or *gobble* is of *gob*. There is a word *fud*, but it's a noun and means either buttocks or a woman's pubic hair. No, fuddle is an orphan of mysterious ancestry, but it does produce the lovely word *fuddler*.

The *Gentleman's Magazine* of 1756 condemned people who 'fuddle away the day with riot and prophaneness', which is doubtless the result of the fact that fuddling-schools have been undocumented since 1680.

You could be dull and go for some all-purpose *bibbery* (drinking establishment), or you could be ambitious and choose a *drunkery* (a place where people get drunk). But it is vital that you start the evening with precision, even though you will in the end arrive at that dread place written of in the *Western Canadian dictionary and phrase-book: things a newcomer wants to know* (1912):

Snake-room, a side room of a basement where saloon-keepers accommodate doped or drunken people until they recover their senses, presumably a place where they 'see snakes'.

In fact, it may be worthwhile to enquire about the facilities in the snake-room before you even go through the door with your *snecklifter*.

Lifting the sneck

A *lanspresado* is (according to a 1736 dictionary of thieves' slang):

He that comes into Company with but Two-pence in his Pocket.

You either know a lanspresado, or you are one. I have taken the latter course.

Lanspresados are everywhere. They have usually forgotten their wallets or can't find a cashpoint (did you know that in Wisconsin cashpoints are called *time machines*?) or some intensely complicated thing has happened with their rent, which means that they're skint till Thursday.

A lanspresado was originally a *lancepesato* or broken lance, who did the work of a corporal without getting a corporal's pay. However, if you want a more English-sounding term you may turn to the snecklifter.

You see, a lanspresado has to prowl around. He goes to the pub, but of course he can't approach the bar unless he sees a friend already there. So he lifts the latch of the pub door, pokes his head in, sees if there's someone who'll buy him a drink, and if there isn't he walks calmly away.

An old word for a latch is a *sneck*, and so a snecklifter is a person who pokes his head into the pub to see if there's anyone who might stand him a little drink.

Called to the bar

Once in the door, sprint straight for the bar, if necessary employing your whiffler (see Chapter 4). Having clubbed your way through the throng, gesticulate wildly and shriek for service. The best way of getting noticed by the bar staff is to call them by unusual names. A man might positively resent being called 'barkeep' but hurry to serve somebody who addressed him as *Squire of the Gimlet* (1679) or *Knight of the Spigot* (1821). Similarly, a lady of the bar may be called (and apparently was called in the eighteenth century) a *pandoratrix*, on the basis that she, like the Pandora of mythology, has all the world's delights and diseases for sale. However, a more poetic name for a barmaiden is *Hebe*, which the OED neatly defines as:

> 1. The goddess of youth and spring, represented as having been originally the cup-bearer of Olympus; hence applied *fig.* to:
> a. A waitress, a barmaid.

The male equivalent of a Hebe (pronounced *HE-be*) would be a *Ganymede*, which has a similar sort of definition:

> 1. A cup-bearer, a youth who serves out liquor; humorously, a pot-boy.

But they might balk at:

    2. A catamite.

So it's best to leave mythology out of it and stick to something matey like *birler* or *bombard man*. Only if they fail to serve you within thirty seconds should you start hurling abuse at them. If it comes to that, *under-skinker* is a good Shakespearean word, but is unequal to the cruel contempt contained in the term *lickspiggot*.

Ordering

Once you have the *tapster*'s attention it is time to actually order your drinks. First, check to see whether there's a female present who wants brandy. If there is, you can say that she's a *bingo-mort*, and provided that the barman is fluent in the thieves' dialect of the eighteenth century, where *bingo* was brandy and a *mort* was a woman, then you'll be served straight away. Such fluency will also allow you to insist on a *soldier's bottle* (a large one) rather than a *bawdy house bottle* (a very small one), because even three hundred years ago they were trying to rip people off in such bars.

Gin may be referred to as *strip me naked*, but this should be done with caution as the tapster may take you at your word, so you might be better off asking for a glass of *royal poverty*. The same caution should be applied when referring to whisky as *spunkie*, or to strong beer as *nappy ale* (on the basis that it makes you want to take a nap).

It may be simplest to ask for *stagger-juice* all round and see
what happens. After all, all that is really required is a memory-
dulling *nepenthe*, a drink to make you forget. Or you may
simply quote the Bible to the barman, the 31st chapter of the
Book of Proverbs to be precise:

> Give strong drink unto him that is ready to perish, and wine
> unto those that be of heavy hearts. Let him drink, and forget
> his poverty, and remember his misery no more.

Fuddling

Ah, the sweet *guggle* of drink poured forth! The OED insists that
drink guggles from a bottle, but it's a matter of onomatopoeic
choice really. And ah, the happiness of the corner of the bar (or
snuggery) to which you retire with your hard-won potations.
Snuggery – despite its obvious rhymes of *thuggery*, *skulduggery*
and *humbuggery* – is one of the pleasantest words in the English
language.

Every pub used to have a snuggery of some sort or another,
and they had supernatural qualities. A nineteenth-century
Scottish writer observed that:

> The Snuggery, sir, has a power o' contraction an' expansion,
> that never belonged afore to any room in this sublunary world.
> Let the pairty be three or thretty, it accommodates its dimen-
> sions to the gatherin'.

Within the snuggery not only are the rules of sublunar space relaxed, but all human endeavours, all that mankind has ever fought, strived and died for is suddenly achieved without the slightest effort. Elsewhere on this petty orb, people are fighting and demonstrating and revolting and campaigning to achieve an equality that is somehow assumed in the snuggery over a few pints. Lord and commoner, billionaire and beggar, senior vice president in charge of sales and junior intern in charge of tea; all sit in parity around the beer mats. Cares, sorrows and injustices are abandoned somewhere near the till and all are equally jolly (except the nicotinians who have to go outside these days).

Of course, the table will probably require *pooning*. It usually does. To poon is:

> To prop up the piece of furniture with a wedge (a poon) under
> the leg (from 1856). Originally, to poon seems to have meant to
> be unsteady, and you propped up the leg that pooned.

That definition is taken from a dictionary of school slang peculiar to the Collegium Sancta Maria Wincorum or, in the common tongue, St Mary's College of Winchester. It seems astonishing that an action so bloody universal should have a name only in one boarding school in the nether regions of Hampshire, but that's how language works. Your dinner table probably needed to be pooned as well, but it was less necessary when the glasses were less full. Not that they will be full for long.

The results of fuddling

Once you are properly *vinomadefied* all sorts of intriguing things start to happen. Vinomadefied, by the way, does not mean 'made mad by wine', but merely dampened by it. It's the sister word of *madefied* meaning moistened, and on the other side of the family is a relative of *vinolent*, which has nothing to do with violence and merely means:

> Addicted to drinking wine, tending to drunkenness.

It's a word that the Wife of Bath used in her grand and gaudy prologue:

> For all so siker [surely] as cold engendereth hail,
> A lickerous mouth must han [have] a lickerous tail.
> In women vinolent is no defence –
> This knowen lechers by experience.

Which may be rewritten for these more modern, more enlightened, post-feminist times as:

> From lecherous women there is no defence
> Especially when you're feeling vinolent.

But to return to the subject: vinomadefied is just a finer, more Latinate way of saying *beer-sodden* or *ale-washed*.

Once the vino has begun to madefy you, you may find that your hand becomes rather *wankle*, or unsteady. In fact, it may not even be your hand that's unsteady, just everything around it; after all, Thomas of Erceldonne noticed right back in the fifteenth century that 'Þe worlde is wondur wankill'.

The result of wankle hands is that whatever you're fuddling tends to divide itself neatly between your mouth, where it should be, and your nice clean top, where it shouldn't. The resulting spots were called *the tears of the tankard* by eighteenth-century drinkers, and in the messier officer's messes of the Second World War they were called *canteen medals*, on the basis that they tend to end up just where the silverware would on parade day.

There are, though, worse stains than the tankard's tears that can befall a fuddler through no fault of their own. Sailors used to refer to the

ADMIRAL OF THE NARROW SEAS. One who, from drunkenness, vomits into the lap of the person sitting opposite him.

This is pretty bad, and can ruin the whole atmosphere of the snuggery. However, it gets worse. Or at least it does if you take your shoes off while you're drinking. I assume that sailors used to drink barefoot – if not I can find no reasonable explanation for the following definition, which seems downright ungentlemanly:

VICE ADMIRAL OF THE NARROW SEAS. A drunken man that pisses under the table into his companions' shoes.

I mean, damn it all. That's hardly what you want to greet a probing toe at the end of the evening. Also, I don't quite see how one could manage to be a Vice Admiral of the Narrow Seas unless one had first picked up the shoe, or had quite fantastic aim beneath the table. There is no equivalent phrase for ladies, nor is there likely to be (even though there is, in the OED, an *admiraless*, meaning either a female admiral or the wife of a male one).

Arriving at the island

> ISLAND. He drank out of the bottle till he saw the island; the island is the rising bottom of a wine bottle, which appears like an island in the centre, before the bottle is quite empty.

Napoleon was not more sorry to spy St Helena, or Dreyfuss to sight Devil's Island, than the keen drinker is to see that dreaded lump appear out of the wine-dark sea. At this point it must be decided by those around the table whether this is an ordinary drink or one to be consumed *supernaculum*. *Super* is Latin for on, and *nagel* is German for fingernail, and like this odd combination, drinking supernaculum is a rather odd custom described in 1592 thus:

> Drinking super nagulum, a device of drinking new come out of France: which is, after a man hath turned up the bottom of his cup, to drop it on his nail and make a pearl with that is left which, if it slide & he cannot make stand on, by reason there's too much, he must drink again for his penance.

Supernaculum can either be an adverb, as above, or a noun to describe a drink so fine that not a drop is to be wasted. So a couple of hundred years later a dictionary simply defines it as:

Supernaculum, good liquor, of which there is not even a drop left sufficient to wet one's nail.

And a hundred years later it had become a toast or drinking cry. The novelist/Prime Minister Benjamin Disraeli has a description of a drinking contest in his first novel *Vivian Grey* (1827):

> The cup was now handed across the table to the Baron Asmanshausen. His Lordship performed his task with ease; but as he withdrew the horn from his mouth, all present, except Vivian, gave a loud cry of 'Supernaculum!' The Baron smiled with great contempt, as he tossed, with a careless hand, the great horn upside downwards, and was unable to shed upon his nail even the one excusable pearl.

The Baron was drinking a bottle of the finest Johannisberger, which is definitely a supernaculum drink. If you have been sipping at something less, then you should perhaps not get it down to the last drop. Instead, leave it to be mixed up in a bucket to be consumed by the poor of the parish. These mixed up *heel-taps* are known as *alms drinks* and go to people living in alms houses, although they're mentioned in Shakespeare as a quickfire way of getting somebody horribly, horribly plastered. Either way, whether you have pursued the Baron's path or the Christian one, you should now see a *marine officer* standing on the table.

> MARINE OFFICER. An empty bottle: marine officers being held useless by the seamen.

Well, that was the reasoning given in a dictionary of 1811. But come 1860 another slang dictionary has a different explanation.

> MARINE, or MARINE RECRUIT, an empty bottle. This expression having once been used in the presence of an officer of marines, he was at first inclined to take it as an insult, until some one adroitly appeased his wrath by remarking that no offence could be meant, as all that it could possibly imply was, 'one who had done his duty, and was ready to do it again.'

Ready to do it again? Splendid. But first, how drunk are you?

The stately progress of the drinker

The standard modern measurement of inebriation is the *Ose* system. This has been considerably developed over the years, but the common medical consensus currently has *jocose, verbose, morose, bellicose, lachrymose, comatose, adios.*

This is a workable but incomplete system, as it fails to take in *otiose* (meaning impractical) which comes just after jocose. Nor does it have *grandiose* preceding bellicose. And how they managed to miss out *globose* (amorphous or formless) before comatose is beyond me.

Back in the sixteenth century, medicine was a much less developed science. Still, in 1592 a chap called Thomas Nashe produced a good diagnostic system of the eight stages of drunkenness.

> Nor have we one or two kinds of drunkards only, but eight kinds.

The first is ape drunke; and he leapes, and singes, and hollowes, and danceth for the heavens;

The second is lion drunke; and he flings the pots about the house, calls his hostesse whore, breakes the glasse windowes with his dagger, and is apt to quarrell with anie man that speaks to him;

The third is swine drunke; heavie, lumpish, and sleepie, and cries for a little more drinke, and a fewe more cloathes;

The fourth is sheepe drunk; wise in his conceipt, when he cannot bring foorth a right word;

The fifth is mawdlen drunke; when a fellowe will weepe for kindnes in the midst of ale, and kisse you, saying, 'By God, captaine, I love thee. Goe thy wayes; thou dost not thinke so often of me as I doo thee; I would (if it pleased God) I could not love thee as well as I doo;' and then he puts his finger in his eye, and cryes;

The sixt is Martin[1] drunke; when a man is drunke, and drinkes himselfe sober ere he stirre;

The seventh is goate drunke; when, in his drunkennes, he hath no minde but on lecherie;

The eighth is fox drunke – when he is craftie drunke, as manie of the Dutchmen bee, that will never bargaine but when they are drunke.

---

[1] The *Martin* here may be a Pine Marten, or it may be an unidentified kind of monkey, or it may be an obscure reference to the Martin Marprelate controversy in which Nashe was involved and which is much too complicated to explain here.

All these species, and more, I have seen practised in one company at one sitting; when I have been permitted to remain
sober amongst them, only to note their several humours.

Animals have a strange knack of wandering into descriptions
of drunkenness, which is odd when you think about it, as they
rarely get served in pubs. And owls: the *Chambers Slang Dictionary*
has a whole entry on the different sorts of owl that you can be
as drunk as, without ever explaining how a 'fresh-boiled owl'
could be drunk at all, or why anybody would have boiled it.

The Aztecs (when not sacrificing humans) had an even
more wonderfully whimsical system of animal-based drunkenness. They used rabbits. Four hundred rabbits – the *Centzon
Totochtin*.

When the Aztecs fermented the sap of the maguey plant (or
Agave americana) they got a milky-looking drink called *pulque*,
which got them nice and tiddly. Therefore, in Aztec mythology, when Mayahuel, the goddess of the maguey plant, married
Patecatl, the god of fermentation, she gave birth to four hundred divine rabbits, which she fed from her four hundred divine
breasts.

These four hundred heavenly rabbits would meet for regular pulque-swilling parties, and were pretty much permanently
pissed. A couple of their names are recorded – Ometochtli (or
'Rabbit No. 2') and Macuiltochtli (or 'Rabbit No. 5') – and,
frankly, the rest can be guessed.

The point of all this is that the Aztecs measured drunkenness in rabbits. Fifteen rabbits was, apparently, ideal. But if you
were four hundred rabbits then you were completely gone. A
lovely little coda to this story is that though the conquistadors

stamped out the native religion, they never managed to quite stamp on the boozy bunnies. That's why there is, to this day, a Mexican phrase: 'As drunk as four hundred rabbits.'

There are uncountable terms for being drunk. Benjamin Franklin (when not taking the air baths described in Chapter 2 or writing interesting essays like *Fart Proudly*) observed that most vices have pleasant names. So misers can claim that they are being thrifty, spendthrifts that they are generous, lechers that they are passionate. But 'Drunkenness is a very unfortunate vice; in this respect it bears no kind of similitude to any sort of virtue, from which it might possibly borrow a name; and is therefore reduced to the wretched necessity of being expressed by round about phrases [...] Though every one may possibly recollect a dozen at least of these expressions, used on such occasions, yet I think no one who has not much frequented taverns could imagine the number of them to be so great as it really is.' So for the sake of the drunkards of posterity he made a list of over two hundred synonyms for sozzled.[2] It contains some beer-sodden gems. Back then a drinker could be *jambled*, *nimtopsical*, *super nonsensical*, *wise or otherwise* or *as drunk as a wheelbarrow*. He could delicately be said to have *smelt an onion*, or he could move up the social scale and have *made too free with Sir John Strawberry* and announce that *Sir Richard has taken off his considering cap*. Unfortunately there are no explanations included in Franklin's dictionary and we'll never know who Sir Richard might originally have been. However, for one of his phrases – *as drunk as David's sow* – there is a complete explication in Captain Grose's *Dictionary of the Vulgar Tongue*:

---

[2] The list in its entirety may be found in an Appendix at the back of the book.

As drunk as David's sow; a common saying, which took its rise from the following circumstance: One David Lloyd, a Welchman, who kept an alehouse at Hereford, had a living sow with six legs, which was greatly resorted to by the curious; he had also a wife much addicted to drunkenness, for which he used sometimes to give her due correction. One day David's wife having taken a cup too much, and being fearful of the consequences, turned out the sow, and lay down to sleep herself sober in the stye. A company coming in to see the sow, David ushered them into the stye, exclaiming, there is a sow for you! did any of you ever see such another? all the while supposing the sow had really been there; to which some of the company, seeing the state the woman was in, replied, it was the drunkenest sow they had ever beheld; whence the woman was ever after called David's sow.

But though David's wife may have appeared bedraggled to the company, I'm sure the company looked lovely to her, as she would have been wearing *beer-goggles*. Sober people always appear much prettier to drunkards than drunkards appear to the sober – and this is one of the chief advantages of inebriation: the elimination of ugliness. The psychological term for this is *kalopsia*: a wonderful form of madness whereby everything becomes beautiful.

It is enough to fill your head with *lovethoughts*, for as Shakespeare rightly observed, alcohol 'provokes the desire'. So perhaps now is the time to do something about it.

Chapter 17

10 p.m. – Wooing

*On the prowl – observing your target – the chat-up
– dancing – kissing – making rash proposals of marriage
– fanfreluching – rejection*

❧

Now that you are thoroughly tanked up, it's probably time to attempt to mate, as it's well known that true love is merely a peculiarly painful sort of drunkenness. And anyway, it's *dragging time*, helpfully defined in the *Dictionary of Obsolete and Provincial English* as 'The evening of a fair day when the lads pull the wenches about'.

The dictionaries, though, are usually unkind to lovers. They tend to have all sorts of rude words like *lecher* or *slattern* that seem designed to make somebody ashamed of their natural obscene urges.

A much more pleasant term is *fleshling*, which the OED defines, rather coyly, as 'a fleshly minded person'. Fleshling sounds a little like *duckling* and a little like *gosling* and altogether makes you seem as innocent as a newborn baby. It's certainly a lot nicer than this definition in a late seventeenth-century dictionary of slang:

Mutton-Monger, a Lover of Women; also a Sheep-stealer.

However, if you flick a few pages back through that same dictionary you'll find a much more civilised term:

> *Give Nature a Fillip*, to Debauch a little now and then with Women, or Wine.

A *fillip*, incidentally, is the little movement you get if you brace the tip of a finger against your thumb and then release it. As that's a good way of tossing a coin to somebody, fillip came to refer to any little gift or treat.

A few pages onwards you find the true rustic joy of:

> *Green-Gown*, a throwing of young Lasses on the Grass, and Kissing them.

Ah, the beauties of a good dictionary! But before such herbaceous hedonism you will first have to find yourself a lass or lad, not to mention a comfortable lawn.

On the prowl

So you must set out into the great fleshy unknown to find yourself somebody to call your own, or at least to call when you're lonely. You must wander about on the pull. There are all sorts of delightful terms for this. In the seventeenth century you would have been:

> *Proling*, Hunting or Searching about in quest of a Wench, or any Game.

In the eighteenth century:

> **Caterwauling** Going out in the night in search of intrigues, like a cat in the gutters.

And in the nineteenth:

> OUT ON THE PICKAROON. Picarone is *Spanish* for a thief, but this phrase does not necessarily mean anything dishonest but ready for anything in the way of excitement to turn up; also to be in search of anything profitable.

And in Scotland you would have *sprunted*, or you would if you could find a convenient haystack:

> To SPRUNT, v, n, To run among the stacks after the girls at night

However, I contend that the best possible term for pootling around on the lookout for a lover is *Ogo-Pogoing*. This will require some explanation.

If you ask the average person what an Ogo-Pogo is, they will tell you to get stuffed. If, however, you ask somebody from British Columbia, they will tell you that the Ogo-Pogo is a sort of monster that lives in the Okanagan Lake and occasionally poses for extremely grainy photographs. It is, in short, the Canadian answer to the Loch Ness Monster. However, even they are unlikely to know that the real name of this unreal beast was Naitaka, and that Ogo-Pogo is a nickname taken from a British music-hall song that was a big hit in the 1920s.

It's a catchy tune, and it seems that people still remembered it in 1939, when pilots in the Royal Air Force would be sent out to fly around Britain on the off-chance that they would spot an enemy aircraft. The RAF pilots called this Ogo-Pogoing, presumably because while winging around scanning the skies they would sing to themselves the refrain from the song: 'I'm looking for the Ogo-Pogo/The funny little Ogo-Pogo.'

So Ogo-Pogo started out as a nonsense song, became the name of a mythical Canadian beast, and was taken up by the RAF meaning to fly around on the off-chance of meeting somebody. It would be a catastrophe if a word with such a rich history were to decline into disuse. And how better to describe the hopeless search for that mythical beast called Love? You even have, thanks to the RAF, the possibilities of sudden destruction or timeless glory built in. As tempting as the idea of proling, caterwauling, pickarooning or even sprunting may be, Ogo-Pogoing is without a doubt the finest word for wandering around with vague hopes of love.

Observing the prey

It is never easy to find a suitable target while Ogo-Pogoing. Many a female who sees the *Oxford English Dictionary*'s definition of *spanandry* – 'Lack or extreme scarcity of males in a population' – is liable to let out an all too familiar sigh. When you want a man, every party and every nightclub is dispiritingly spanandrous. In fact, one's *dioestrus* (a short period of sexual inactivity for females) can suddenly seem to stretch out into eternity.

But then it begins, very quietly, with a little *propassion*. A propassion is the first stirring of a proper passion, or indeed merely the feeling that there's a passion somewhere on its way, and that suffering is not far off. Our word passion, meaning love, as we saw in Chapter 1, derives from the Latin for suffering, on the simple basis that the two are one and the same; so the Passion of the Christ (his suffering upon the cross) is the same as our petty romantic passions, etymologically speaking.

For the moment you may merely *smicker*; it's a good way to start. To smicker is 'to look amorously or wantonly at or after a person', usually after, of course, although a glossary of medieval Scottish poetry (there are such things) says that to *smikker* is to 'smile in a seducing manner'. Either way, if you smicker enough you may well develop an acute *smickering*, or amorous inclination, towards someone. Smickering was a favourite word of John Dryden, who came up with the lovely line:

Must you be smickering after wenches while I am in calamity?

You can even smicker in very precise ways. For example, you may be particularly drawn to a pair of dark eyes, or a shapely nose, or an intriguing ankle. Those who study sexual attraction for a living (legally) call this *agastopia*, an immensely useful word that is defined in the *Descriptive Dictionary and Atlas of Sexology* thus:

Agastopia. A rarely used term for admiration of any particular part of the body.

Why it should be rarely used is a mystery, as agastopia was known even to the sexologists and sculptors of the ancient world. It is from the bottom-fond Greeks that we get the modern English term *callipygian*, meaning beautiful-buttocked.

There was a whole cult in ancient Syracuse devoted to Aphrodite Kallipygos, or Venus of the Beautiful Bottom, or at least there may have been. The only description we have of it comes from an ancient Greek chap called Alciphron who spent his time composing imaginary letters.

It is certain that the Greeks would commission all sorts of sculptures of callipygian Venus in which the main purpose was to make her as lovely-bottomed as possible. Lucian of Samosata records seeing one such statue carved by the greatest sculptor of antiquity: Praxiteles. This statue, apparently, was rather too good. So sexy was Aphrodite's posterior that a young man was discovered in the temple committing enthusiastic blasphemy with the marble goddess. He was rather embarrassed by this, as I suppose you would be, and cast himself into the sea. But though he died, the term callipygian lived on, and it can of course be applied to both sexes, mortal and immortal, marble and flesh.

But to move on from such *natiform* (or buttock-shaped) delights, one's agastopia might instead be directed at the *bathy-colpian*. Bathycolpian means 'deep-bosomed' and is an absurdly oblique and beautiful way of saying that a lady has voluptu-ous and luxuriant breasts. The advantages of describing a lady in such an incomprehensible manner will be evident to anyone who has ever been slapped or released on strict parole.

With all these different body parts to glance at, it is no wonder that you move your eyes from side to side using the *amatorial* muscles. One eighteenth-century dictionary is quite unnecessarily precise about it:

> AMATORII *Musculi* [among Anatomists] Muscles of the Eyes, which give them a Cast sideways, and assist that particular look called Ogling.

And there we have the problem. You are fast becoming an *ogler*, a *snilcher*, a *haker*. And if you thought hake was only a kind of fish:

> HAKE: To hanker after, to gape after, to sneak or loiter.

You must up your game if you do not wish to be thought merely a *gazehound* and amorous gongoozler. If you have decided upon your intended, it is high time that you did something about it. If you are a lady, you may give a coy *arrision* (which is the act of smiling at somebody) or practise your *minauderie* (coquettish manner). If you are a man, and you have picked out your *rum-strum* (a highwayman's term for a handsome wench) it may be time to *pavonize*, or act like a peacock showing off your magnificent tail in order to cow all the potential peahens with your magnificent masculinity.

But there's no use in just pavonizing; one is in danger of being a mere *dangler* ('To dangle – To follow a woman around without asking the question'). You must decide if this is a grand passion or a mere *velleity*, which the OED sternly defines as 'The fact or quality of merely willing, wishing, or desiring, without any effort or advance towards action or realization'.

Of course there may be reasons for your inaction. Perhaps the object of your affections is a *figurant*. This is, I confess, a technical balletic term for somebody who dances only in a group and never by themselves, but its usefulness in the discotheque should be self-evident. It is extraordinarily hard to sidle up to a figurant who has enclosed themselves within a protective fortification of bouncing shoulders and turned backs, but it must be attempted. Faint heart never won fair rum-strum.

You may even be covered in what the Old English liked to call *need-sweat*, which is the perspiration caused by acute anxiety. But what is such sweat compared with *anuptaphobia*, the morbid terror of remaining single? Though anuptaphobia is only a psychological term, she really should be a goddess, a cruel and terrible deity who directs all of humanity's most embarrassing actions. For who can disobey when Anuptaphobia commands? It is time to approach the object of your mute affections. And if Anuptaphobia tells you to *flichter* to him or her, then you must flichter.

And in case you were wondering:

FLICHTER v. To run with outspread arms, like a tame goose half-flying; applied to children, when running to those to whom they are much attached. [Dumfries dialect] Hence:

FLICHTER-FAIN adj. So fond of an object as to run to it in the manner above described.

The simplest methods are often the most effective.

The chat-up

Each species has its own particular mating call. A badger, for example, *shrikes* to his would-be beloved. A fox *clickets*. A goat *rattles*. A deer *croons*. A sow *breems* for her pig. A cow *eassins* for her bull. And an otter *whineth*. You should do none of these and if you hear a shrike, make your excuses and leave, as you are dealing with a badger in disguise.

Luckily for all of us, the correct way to initiate conversation has already been discovered and set down in writing by Christopher Marlowe:

> Come live with me and be my love
> And we will all those pleasures prove
> That hills and valleys, dale and field,
> And all the craggy mountains yield.

If that doesn't work, or if your intended expresses a distaste for craggy mountains, you could go for the 1950s standard: 'Suppose we get together and split a herring.' Unfortunately, everybody in the 1950s was too hep to record why it was a herring that needed splitting. A more explicable term was recorded by Cab Calloway: 'Wouldst like to con a glimmer with me this early black?', which he helpfully explains as 'the proper way to ask a young lady to go to the movies'. It should be noted here, that if the object of your affections replies 'Kill me', they are not requesting to be euthanatised and you should not actually murder them. *Kill me* is merely the Cab Calloway way of saying 'Show me a good time' and is the best response you could have hoped for. Jive was rather confusing in this way. *Murder* is defined in the *Hepsters Dictionary* as 'Something excellent or terrific', which is all very well provided that both parties are familiar with the idiolect, but it might lead to confusion and a rather feeble-sounding excuse in court.

Or one could go down the simpler route of throwing out a compliment or two. If you do so, you must try to be a little more gentlemanly than Dr Johnson was in his dictionary. In a rare moment of misogyny he wrote:

> **Bellibone** n. A woman excelling in both beauty and goodness.
> A word now out of use.

According to the OED the word was last used in 1586, which makes one wonder what occurred in 1587 that made ladies one or the other and rendered *bellibone* redundant.

Alternatively, you could call a lady a *wonder wench* (an old Yorkshire term for a sweetheart) or, if you're feeling ready to defend yourself, *cowfyne*, which even in a dictionary of Scottish terms is defined as 'a ludicrous term of endearment'. In fact, the only proper riposte that a lady can give to being called cowfyne is to reply that the chap is *snoutfair*, which means handsome, although the OED notes that it is usually used 'with some disparaging suggestion'.

What, though, if your initial blandishments and entreaties are met not with a flirtatious exchange of archaic endearments, but with indifference, incredulity, contemptuous laughter or sudden flight? Fear not. This may merely be a case of *accismus*.

Accismus is a rhetorical term meaning pretended lack of interest in that which you keenly desire.

Foolish Accismus hath a qualitie
To deny offer'd things in modestie:

Accismus was once considered the most necessary virtue of the female. For example, there's a rather peculiar polemic against girls' schools from the Victorian period that asserts:

> A woman requires no figure of eloquence – herself excepted – so often as that of *accismus* ... On this account, mothers, fathers, men, and even youths, are their best companions; on the contrary, girls connected with other girls of a similar age, as in schools, provoke one another to an exchange of foibles, rather than of excellences, to a love of dress, admiration, and gossip, even to the forgetting of *accismus*.

But of course all of this raises the question of when accismus (male or female) is really accismus, and when (dare I broach the possibility?) it is true uninterest. This is a question that has puzzled young lovers through the ages, but which was long ago solved by the Church of England through the system of Nolo Episcopari.

Appointing a bishop is a tricky business. To be a bishop you have to possess the Christian virtue of humility; however, if you actually are humble you'll probably think that you're not worthy of being a bishop and turn the job down. Even if you secretly think that you'd make a splendid bishop and would look marvellous in a mitre, you can't just come out and say it. It would look bad. So you had to practise a little bit of accismus by announcing in front of the assembled company of churchmen that you'd really rather not become a bishop, or, in Latin, 'Nolo episcopari'.

When you had solemnly announced this, rather than saying 'Oh well, that's that, I suppose', the church council would ask you a second time, and for a second time you would humbly reply 'Nolo episcopari'. On the third go, you would say, 'Oh all right then, go on' or 'Volo episcopari' or somesuch line of assent. You would thus have displayed your humility and got the job.

However, it is dreadfully important to keep count, as if you said 'Nolo episcopari' a third time it would be assumed that you really meant it and your chances of promotion would be for ever scuppered. It's rather like the Rule of the Bellman described by Lewis Carroll in *The Hunting of the Snark*: 'What I tell you three times is true.'

Hope as you might, three cases of accismus are definitive and after that you deserve a slap.

This is often the stage of courtship where a woman wishes she were equipped with a *parabore*, or defence against bores. It is uncertain what a parabore would look like, although in the first (and only) usage recorded in the OED it is described as:

> … a Bore-net, a para-bore, to protect me, like our musquito-
> curtains

So a parabore could perhaps be attached to a wide-brimmed hat. You could have some sort of rip-cord device, which when pulled would drop a thick veil around the whole head in the manner of a beekeeper. Thus, with a flick of the wrist, the belea-guered belle could make herself vanish from view and give a stern and certain message to her suitor. If parabores could be manufactured for a reasonable cost I imagine that they would become quite popular, though dispiriting to the poor chap who sees a whole group of girls reach for their rip-cords at his timorous approach.

If this unhappy fate does befall you, you can keep some semblance of honour by turning again to the dictionary of Hepster slang and crying, 'You're a V-8, baby, a V-8', where a *V-8* is, for some reason, 'A chick that spurns company'. However, it may be best not to get into an exchange of insults, as (from behind her thick veil) she could throw some hurtful barbs of her own. A few suggestions might be:

> **Twiddle-Poop** An effeminate looking man
> **Smell-smock** A licentious man

Or, most terrible of all, this from Dr Johnson's dictionary:

> **Amatorcultist**. n.s. [amatorculus, Lat.] A little, insignificant lover; a pretender to affection.

There is no coming back from being called an amatorcultist; all you can do is dwindle away and disappear in a shower of tears.

But let us assume some little success at this early amatory stage. Where now? It's a fifty-fifty chance that your main aim is to be *thelyphthoric*, a word that comes from the Greek *thely* meaning 'woman' and *phthoric* meaning 'corrupting', thus the OED's simple definition: 'that corrupts or ruins women'.

Thelyphthoric began its life in English as the title of a smashing 1780 treatise:

THELYPHTHORA; OR, A TREATISE ON FEMALE RUIN, IN
ITS CAUSES, EFFECTS, CONSEQUENCES, PREVENTION,
AND REMEDY; CONSIDERED ON THE BASIS OF THE
DIVINE LAW: Under the following HEADS, viz. MARRIAGE,
WHOREDOM, FORNICATION, ADULTERY, POLYGAMY,
and DIVORCE; With many other Incidental Matters.

It's a promising title, and it gets better with the first sentence:
'The Author doth not scruple to call this TREATISE, one of
the most important and interesting Publications, that have
appeared since the Days of the *Protestant Reformation*.'

But as you read further (and who wouldn't?) it turns out that
far from being a useful instruction manual, the author is dead
against female ruin and all the accompanying pleasantness for
both parties. In fact, he has a high moral purpose of preventing
female ruin through the outlawing of divorce and the reintro-
duction of polygamy.

Thelyphthoric didn't keep its high moral tone for long and
instead tobogganed off into the linguistic lowlands. Frankly, a
word like that is never going to remain in the purest of hands,
especially as most of the world's population either want to be
thelyphthoric or be introduced to somebody who is.

The dance-floor

The most common way of attempting thelyphthora is to dance,
jig, *shake a hough*, or *tripudiate*. The thelyphthoric qualities of
such rhythmic movements are amply recorded in the dictionaries. For example, from the eighteenth century:

Balum-Rancum A hop or dance, where the women are all prostitutes. N.B. The company dance in their birthday suits.

Or from the other perspective:

Gymnopaedic *Ancient Greek Hist.* The distinctive epithet of the dances or other exercises performed by naked boys at public festivals.

Or for both sexes:

Among the tramping fraternity a *buff-ball* is a dancing party, characterised by the indecency of those who attend it, the *costume de rigueur* being that of our first parents.

The most favourite entertainment at this place is known as '*buff-ball*,' in which both sexes – innocent of clothing – madly join, stimulated with raw whisky and the music of a fiddle and a tin-whistle.

But how to suggest such a thing in a manner both alluring and learned? In the 1960 film *Beat Girl*, Oliver Reed approaches a stylish young she-cat sitting in a bar and says: 'Say, baby, you feel terpsichorical? Let's go downstairs and fly.' Terpsichore is one of the nine ancient muses, and specifically the muse who inspires dancing. So Mr Reed's enquiry, in the context of the film, means: 'Do you feel inspired by the muse of dance? Let us go to the basement and do just that.' And, in the context of the film, it works. How or why Terpsichore got so famous in the mid-twentieth century is a bit of a mystery, but the OED even records the shortened verb *to terp*.

But what if you are not inspired by the moving muse? If you have not paid her sufficient sacrifices she may curse you with a flip of her immortal foot and leave you *baltering* upon the dance-floor. *Balter* is an old verb meaning to dance clumsily, although one dictionary defines it strictly as 'to tread in a clownish manner, as an ox does the grass'.

Make me immortal with a kiss

The Yaghan people of Tierra Del Fuego at the southernest tip of South America were one of the few tribes ever discovered who didn't wear clothes. This is not because Tierra Del Fuego is a warm and balmy place. It is not. Even in summer the temperature rarely rises above nine degrees centigrade. Yet naked they were, even when Charles Darwin visited them on the *Beagle* and, rather impolitely, called them 'miserable, degraded savages'. It would appear that the Yaghans simply hadn't invented clothing, but they did have an ingenious method for keeping warm, which was to smear themselves head to toe in grease and cuddle each other. This ingenious and energy-efficient practice must be kept in mind when considering their insanely useful word *mamihlapinatapai*.

Mamihlapinatapai is usually defined as 'Two people looking at each other each hoping the other will do what both desire but neither is willing to do'. Mamihlapinatapai is therefore generally reckoned to be one of the most useful words on earth. As two people stand at a doorway each gesturing 'After you', that is mamihlapinatapai. As two people sitting in a dull waiting room both hope that the other will start a conversation, that is mamihlapinatapai. And when two people look into each other's eyes, with that sudden realisation that lips can be used for something other than talking, but both too afraid to draw the other to them, that is Mamihlapinatapai Rex.

However, mamihlapinatapai is a rather controversial word. Experts on the Yaghan language (a group of which I cannot claim membership), while conceding that the word is theoretically possible, tend to pooh-pooh the idea that it ever actually existed. It could exist, just as in English the word *antifondlingness* could exist, but that doesn't mean it does. Mamihlapinatapai is, according to them, a whimsical invention of some unknown linguist.

This case looks, at first blush, rather convincing. How could a tribe that hadn't even invented clothes come up with a word so complex? However, I would contend that the two points are in fact connected, because if you spend half your time naked, cuddling and covered in grease, mamihlapinatapai is going to be a pretty common feeling. In fact it would probably be the dominant emotion of your nude, greasy existence.

So let us assume that the dancing is over, that your eyes have met, and that mamihlapinatapai has come upon you. What to do about it?

The simplest answer I can offer is to ask, 'Care for a biscot?', because *biscot* means 'to caress amorously' but the other person may not know that, and everybody likes a biscuit.

Less deceptive would be to ask the other party whether they are *osculable*. Osculable means 'kissable' but is a much more beautiful word. According to the OED, poor osculable has been used only once, in 1893, to describe the Pope. So the word is nearly virginal and should be taken out and shown to the world.

The Latin for to kiss was *osculare,* and the obscure English words thence derived are wonderful. There's an *osculatrix* (a lady who kisses), an *oscularity* (a kiss), and an *osculary* (anything that can and should be kissed, although this was usually a religious relic).

So, an alternative line could be: 'You are an osculary, and this is my religious duty', or somesuch.

And now it is time for the moment not of truth, but of kissing (the two are entirely separate notions). The eyes close. The lips of the lovers meet. *Cataglottism* is usually attempted by one or both parties, for the definition of which we should turn to Blount's *Glossographia* of 1656:

> *Cataglottism,* a kissing with the tongue.

This word, though rare, has survived for centuries. As the great biologist Henry Havelock Ellis[1] observed in 1905:

> The tonic effect of cutaneous excitation throws light on the psychology of the caress ... The kiss is not only an expression of feeling; it is a means of provoking it. Cataglottism is by no means confined to pigeons.

And a good thing too. But one thing leads to another and the tongue is often merely the thin end of the wedge. The moral dangers of kissing were perhaps most eloquently described by Sir Thomas Urquhart in his *Jewel* of 1652.

---

[1] Translating Charles Féré.

Thus for a while their eloquence was mute, and all they spoke was but with the eye and hand, yet so persuasively, by vertue of the intermutual unlimitedness of their visotactil sensation, that each part and portion of the persons of either was obvious to the sight and touch of the persons of both; the visuriency of either, by ushering the tacturiency of both, made the attrectation of both consequent to the inspection of either.

Where *visuriency* means 'the desire to see' and *tacturiency* means 'the desire to fondle'. It is unfair, though, to judge somebody too harshly on their desire to fondle. The OED records a word at once splendid and tragic:

Fondlesome adj. Addicted to fondling.

It beats heroin. But it should be remembered that recidivist fondlers often need treatment much more than they need punishment. If you object, you should never have given them a *fleshment* in the first place.

Once upon a time you trained animals for the hunt by *fleshing* them. If they did what they were supposed to do, you gave them a little morsel of meat to encourage them; if they did not do what they were meant to do, they were denied their fleshment. Exactly the same principle and the same word may be applied to the actions now under consideration. After all, the OED merely defines fleshment as 'the excitement resulting from a first success'. A fleshment may therefore have the unfortunate result of making people go too far too fast. In the current circumstances this could mean one of two things.

Proposing marriage

Mariturient means 'eager to marry' and is derived from the same sort of desiderative verb that gave us *visuriency* and *tacturiency* in the previous section. Maturiency is a relatively common and benign condition that leads to the most blessed state of matrimony and mutual comfort. But in extreme cases it can manifest itself as *gamomania* ('a form of insanity characterised by strange and extravagant proposals for marriage') and it is with the gamomaniacs that we are now concerned.

Every man is occasionally and honourably seized with the desire to make a woman what was called in the seventeenth century his *comfortable importance*, in the eighteenth century his *lawful blanket* and in these fallen and unimaginative days his *wife*. But gamomania goes beyond this.

The first signs may be detectable if he starts mumbling something about your being *fangast*. Fangast is an obsolete Norfolk dialect term meaning 'fit to marry' whose origins are chronically befogged. Few people know the word any more, and for that reason it could be terribly useful. Suppose that your insignificant other were to discover that you had drawn up a table of all your female acquaintances and next to each name had written 'marriage material' or 'not marriage material'. She'd flip her proverbial lid. But 'fangast' and 'not fangast' – unless she's a time-traveller from ancient Norfolk you're in the clear.

If just one other friend knows the word then the two of you can discuss whether somebody is fangast in front of their face with no danger of discovery: 'Have you met my new girlfriend? She's so pretty, and not at all fangast.'

'What?'

'Nothing, darling, nothing.'

But that's not how the gamomaniac thinks. To him (or her) all are fangast. To all will he bring his *subarrhations* (or gifts for a prospective wife). But you have to remember that though gamo, he's still a maniac and must be refused, however osculable. But of course he isn't necessarily a gamomaniac; he may have a title even less honourable, helpfully defined by Dr Johnson:

Fribbler One who professes rapture for a woman, but fears her consent.

Fanfreluching

The other possible result of fondlesome cataglottism is *fanfreluching*, which is another way of saying *swiving*, *meddling*, *melling*, *mollocking*, *wapping*, *flesh-company*, *quaffing*, *carnal confederacy*, *jelly-roll*, *jazz*, *jig-a-jig*, *jockumcloying*, *hot cockles*, *subagitation*, *interunion*, *the Venus exercise*, *the last favour*, *old hat*, *pom-pom*, *poop-noddy*, *Moll Peatley*, *Sir Berkeley*, or in a word: *sex*.

But here we reach something of a crux. First, this is a serious reference work and I am loath to add anything that may subject it to suggestions of levity. Second, there are as many carnal words as there are carnal actions, and one could get horribly bogged down in explaining exactly what is meant by *changing at Baker Street* – added to which my publishers have insisted that they will not stretch to illustrations. But thirdly and most importantly, this is a reference work that must maintain its relevance and usefulness. So the question that must be asked is whether you, dear reader, are going to pull tonight. And as you, dear reader, are the sort of person who reads books on obscure words, I fear that the answer is No.

It could be worse – you could be the sort of person who writes books on obscure words.

So let us sadly and sorrowfully assume that your *supersaliency* is met with an *imparlibidinous* response (that is, your attempting to initiate coitus by leaping upon the beloved is rebuffed by somebody who finds you less desirable than you find them). The course of true love never did leap smooth. There is a reason that you have never heard the word *equinecessary*, and that is that we so rarely are.

Silence and tears

It is important at this point to scrabble for whatever motes of dignity the situation affords. You could pretend, as you ruefully put your socks back on, that it was a mere *passiuncle* or insignificant passion. It may not be true, but none of the best things are. And as your beloved hurries off to obtain a restraining order, you can console yourself that you did at least have a *Pisgah sight*.

When Moses had led the Children of Israel through the wilderness he asked God to allow him to cross the Jordan into the Promised Land. But God would not let him set foot there, only have a glimpse.

> And Moses went up from the plains of Moab unto the mountain of Nebo, to the top of Pisgah, that is over against Jericho.

And the LORD shewed him all the land of Gilead, unto Dan, And all Naphtali, and the land of Ephraim, and Manasseh, and all the land of Judah, unto the utmost sea, And the south, and the plain of the valley of Jericho, the city of palm trees, unto Zoar. And the LORD said unto him, This is the land which I sware unto Abraham, unto Isaac, and unto Jacob, saying, I will give it unto thy seed: I have caused thee to see it with thine eyes, but thou shalt not go over thither.

So Moses the servant of the LORD died there in the land of Moab, according to the word of the LORD. And he buried him in a valley in the land of Moab, over against Bethpeor: but no man knoweth of his sepulchre unto this day.

And from that sad passage English gained the term 'a Pisgah sight', for something glimpsed but never obtained and never obtainable. By a rather extraordinary feat of self-reference, the OED's entry for Pisgah sight mentions its own first editor, Sir James Murray, who 'led to within a Pisgah sight of completion a larger and more scientifically organized work of linguistic reference than Dr Johnson could have produced', but died before he could see his life's labours in print.

All you are left with is a case of *nympholepsy*, which is a longing for the unobtainable that afflicts any shepherd who happens to come across a wood nymph in the course of his work. Such shepherds are never happy again. They pine away. They neglect their sheep and search the woods for the nymph whom they will never find.

So turn for home. It's late anyway, and you have to get up tomorrow I suppose. We generally do. Button yourself up, pretend it never happened and set off, still perhaps humming to yourself that miserable song in which all human sadness is contained:

I'm looking for the Ogo-Pogo
The funny little Ogo-Pogo
His mother was an earwig, his father was a whale
I'm going to put a little bit of salt on his tail,
I want to find the Ogo-Pogo.

Chapter 18

11 p.m. – Stumbling Home

*Setting off – getting lost – falling over
– attempts to sleep outdoors*

❦

The nymphs are departed, last orders have been called, and it is time to go home. Even Cab Calloway, a committed seeker of nocturnal amusements, went home in the end. His *Hepsters Dictionary* has a couple of helpful entries for things to say at *late bright* or the end of the evening:

> **Final** (v.): to leave, to go home. Ex., 'I finaled to my pad' (went to bed); 'We copped a final' (went home).

And:

> **Trilly** (v.): to leave, to depart. Ex., 'Well, I guess I'll trilly.'

But how will you get home? You could share a taxi. The OED insists that a shared taxi is called a *dolmus*, from the Turkish for 'filled'. But where are your *ale-knights* of the Round Table now, your boon companions in the night's struggle? Gone and bloody departed, that's where. Camelot is derelict, and you'll probably have to go home on foot.

If you are extremely lucky, a *white sergeant* may appear:

> A man fetched from the tavern or ale-house by his wife, is said
> to be arrested by the white sergeant.

But given your behaviour in the last chapter, I think that's
unlikely.

Heading home

In the *Canterbury Tales*, Chaucer explains the whole human
condition and search for happiness in terms of a drunk person trying to walk home. The general theme of his musing is
that though we all seek after happiness, we don't always know
where it is, and end up wandering hither and thither pursuing
the things we thought we wanted.

> We faren [fare] as he that drunk is as a mouse.
> A drunk man woot [knows] well he hath an house,
> But he noot [doesn't know] which the right way is thither
> And to a drunk man the way is slidder [slippery].
> And certes in this world so faren we;
> We seeken fast after felicity
> But we goon wrong full often, trewely.

If the way is particularly *slidder*, perhaps you can persuade
somebody to go *agatewards* with you. This charming old piece
of politeness is now confined to dictionaries of obsolete English:

Agate-Wards, adv. To go *agatewards* with any one, to accompany him part of his way home, which was formerly the last office of hospitality towards a guest, frequently necessary even now for guidance and protection in some parts of the country. In Lincolnshire it is pronounced *agatehouse*, and in the North generally *agaterds*.

Gate here is an old term for the public highway. So if you walked somebody agatewards you would accompany them along the dark, narrow, unfrequented lanes where robbers lurked, and then part with them at the wide open highway, where highwaymen lurked. Highwaymen were an altogether better class of thief. There were even

ROYAL SCAMPS. Highwaymen who never rob any but rich persons, and that without ill treating them.

There was also a *royal footpad*, who was just like a royal scamp except that he didn't have a horse. It is unfortunate that modern muggers seem to be universally republican.

Once you could hire a *moon-curser*, a boy who would walk beside you carrying a torch and lighting your way. Obviously, they were in permanent economic competition with moonlight, hence the name. They were not as honourable as royal scamps:

MOONCURSER. A link-boy: link-boys are said to curse the moon, because it renders their assistance unnecessary; these gentry frequently, under colour of lighting passengers over kennels, or through dark passages, assist in robbing them.

So perhaps it is best to be *solivagant*, to wander alone towards your far-off felicity. *Vagari* was Latin for 'wander', and solivagant is only one of the wonderful *vagant* words in the English language. If you wander outside – or *extra* – the bounds of your budget you are being *extravagant*. Indeed, originally extravagant had no financial connotations at all and simply meant 'wandering around too much'. So when Othello was described as 'an extravagant and wheeling stranger/Of here and everywhere', it just meant that he hadn't settled down. You can also be *mundivagant* (wandering the world), *multivagant* (wandering hither and thither), *montivagant* (wandering the mountains), *nemorivagant* ('wandering in the woods and groves'), *nubivagant* (wandering the clouds), and *omnivagant* (wandering absolutely everywhere).

These words are much more useful than they might appear. Aircraft are all nubivagant, gorillas are all nemorivagant, and a holiday in Snowdonia could be described as a montivagant weekend. In fact, one could be simultaneously montivagant, nubivagant, nemorivagant and extravagant simply by taking an expensive holiday in the Lake District.

The word that we need now, however, is *noctivagant*: wandering around at night. You must stumble like a *gyrovague* (or wandering monk), up blind alleys, *twitchels*, and *diverticulums*. You may well find yourself in a trance, but only because a *trance* is an old Scots term for a passage between two buildings. You will wander, *vagulate* and *wharve*; and it's as likely as not that you will end up a *night-foundered vicambulist*, or 'street-walker who has got lost in the darkness'.

At this point, you may wish to ponder the high-flown

concept of *nullibiety*, or state of being nowhere. It's usually used in theology, but can happily be transferred to trying to find your way home after a couple of drinks too many. It's also got a useful sister-word, *nullibiquitous*, which is the exact opposite of ubiquitous and means 'existing nowhere'. Thus you can search your house for your nullibiquitous car keys or whatnot.

Alternatively, you could look around you at the dark and unfamiliar streets and conclude that you had been *pixilated*, a splendid word and the cause of an awful lot of amusing typos in newspapers, if only you can spot them. Pixilated is completely different to *pixelated*. The latter, with an E, is something that happens to people's faces when they appear on television. But pixilated, with an I, means 'led astray by pixies'. It's astonishing, if you read the newspapers carefully, how many criminals have had their faces led astray by the Little Folk.

Pixies are a pest, and the cause of much wild wandering, or *skimbleskamble oberration* as Dr Johnson would have put it, leaving you *dog-weary* and *upon the wheady mile*.

The wheady mile is a very useful concept, defined in Nathan Bailey's *Universal Etymological Dictionary* of 1721 as 'A Mile beyond Expectation, a tedious one. *Shropshire*'. It's that last bit of a journey that goes on much longer than you had planned. Another dictionary calls it 'A mile of an extraordinary length'. This doesn't make much sense if you take it literally, as miles are, ordinarily, a mile long. But in your current state – drunk, weary and heartbroken – it is an utterly comprehensible idea and I wouldn't blame you if you sank to your knees in night-foundered despair.

Devotional habits

When Diocletian entered Alexandria in 298 AD he was in a foul temper. The city had risen up in revolt against him and it had taken several months of siege before they finally gave in and opened the gates to the emperor, who was by now furious. He immediately ordered his legionaries to start killing the citizens and not to stop until his horse was up to its knees in the blood of the Alexandrians. The population of Alexandria was a little under a million at the time. The average human contains about a gallon of blood. This means that the resources available to the Roman soldiers would have been enough for – to use the standard Journalistic Unit of Measurement – an Olympic swimming pool and a half. Diocletian's plan was therefore thoroughly practicable.

Diocletian's horse had other ideas, though, for just as the soldiers were sharpening their swords and getting ready for the fun, the horse went down on its knees and refused to get up. Diocletian took this as an omen from the gods and immediately called off the massacre, thus saving the town. The Alexandrians erected a statue of the horse.[1]

The Victorians had a term for horses that fell to their knees all the time: they were said to have acquired *devotional habits*, on the basis that it looked as though they were kneeling down to pray. It's rather pleasant to imagine that a horse can't go twenty yards without kneeling to thank its creator. Pleasant for humans at least, not so for the horse, who is probably just old and tired

---

[1] It should be noted that many spoilsport historians think this story is much too good to be true.

and ready for the knacker's yard. Nor will anyone blame you if you acquire devotional habits of your own on your pixilated way.

Falling flat on your face

> **To Seel** a Ship is said to *Seel*, when she tumbles suddenly and violent, sometimes to one side, and sometimes to another, when a Wave passes from under her Sides faster than she can drive away with it.
>
> *Universal Etymological Dictionary*, 1721

Towards midnight a person is said to *seel* when they tumble suddenly and violent, sometimes to one side, and sometimes to another, when the pavement passes under their feet faster than they can stumble away with it, too exhausted and too well-refreshed to continue with this wheady mile.

Mischievous Reality notices you seeling and takes the opportunity to turn upside down and back to front. You totter, and before you have a chance even to cry out 'I *labascate*!', which means 'I begin to fall', you're actually falling in a terrible Newtonian *degringolade* onto your face.

Now is the time of *humicubation*: the act of lying on the ground, especially as a form of repentance. As a seventeenth-century bishop sternly observed:

> Fasting and Sackcloth, and Ashes, and Tears, and Humi-cubations, used to be companions of Repentance. Joy may be a Consequent of it, not a Part of it.

Another useful word here may be *spartle*, to wave the limbs around vainly. Spartling is a common companion of evening humicubations, especially when the midnight creatures come curiously closer.

The moon-cursers and the *bug hunters* gather around. You catch a glimpse of the approaching *vespilone*, 'he that carries forth dead bodies in the night to be buried, as they use in time of plague and great sickness', with his *uncuses*, his *corpse-hooks*, his *eternity box* and his *danna-drag* on which the waste of the city is carried out. The Black Ox licks your cheek. The *barguest*, the ghost of broken walls, is watching with Old Split-Foot. The *hircocervus* blows a *mort*. The *donestres* call for you! The *whang-doodle* wails in the Yggdrasil! The skinless *écorchés* cavort! And Aboaddon, the Angel of the Bottomless Pit, beats time while the four hundred drunken rabbits dance an obscene can-can around you.

Now may be the time to indulge in a spot of *xenodocheion-ology*, which is the study of hotels and places to stay the night. There is the possibility of a *sheep bed*, i.e. the grass. But that won't keep away the *sooterkins* (strange, dark creatures said to grow inside Dutch women). Also, there is the question of warmth. If you are lucky enough to live in California all you will need to do is cover yourself with a newspaper, or *California blanket*. Those in chillier climes could knock on a few doors to see if anybody is feeling *xenodochial* – a slightly shorter relative of xenodocheionology that means 'given to putting strangers up for the night'.

Somebody who goes from house to house, even at this time of night, is *circumforaneous*, whether they're an encyclopedia salesman, a burglar or simply have something important to tell you about salvation.

But what is this? Is this *your mascaron*? Is this your own front door?

Chapter 19

Midnight – Nostos

*Making too much noise upon returning
– attempting to work – undressing
– arguing with spouse – falling asleep*

⌒⌒⌒

The *Oxford English Dictionary* insists that *beauty-sleep* is 'the sleep secured before midnight'. So if you're still up, it's too late. Mind you, if you've gone to bed anywhere near a dairy farm, you may be sitting up in bed looking rather startled and consulting this humble, yet precise, reference work to find out what on earth that noise is. Luckily, I can refer you to *The Vocabulary of East Anglia; An Attempt to Record the Vulgar Tongue of the Twin Sister Counties, Norfolk and Suffolk as It Existed In the Last Years of the Eighteenth Century, and Still Exists* (1830). It's a saucy little page-turner of a dictionary filled with fantastical diseases of the turnip and explanations of why an *arseling pole* and a *bed faggot* aren't what you might have suspected.[1] On the subject of midnight it has this entry:

---

[1] Well, a bed-faggot sort of is. It's 'a contemptuous name for a bed-fellow'; but an arseling pole is utterly innocent and is to do with baking.

BULL'S-NOON, s. midnight. The inhabitants of dairy counties can feelingly vouch for the propriety of this term. Their repose is often broken in the dead of night by the loud bellowing of the lord of the herd, who, rising vigorous from his evening rumination, rushes forth on his adventures, as if it were broad noon-day, and *blores* with increased rage and disappointment when he comes to a fence which he cannot break through.

So if you have just woken up, don't worry. It's merely the lord of the herd back from his evening rumination. If, on the other hand, you *are* the lord of the herd, much the worse for wear after your evening rumination, then you should try to make a little less noise coming home.

The nightingale floor

If you wish to assassinate the Lord of Nijo Castle in Kyoto – and who doesn't occasionally have strange whims? – several diffi-culties will immediately present themselves to you. There are two rings of fortified wall, two rings of moats, and there hasn't actually been a lord there since 1939. However, even once you've surmounted these problems, you're going to have to deal with the *nightingale floor*.

The Tokugawa Shogunate were not the sort of chaps who took chances. So even if you made it to the sleeping quarters, all the floorboards were specially designed to squeak when you walked on them, meaning that you couldn't surprise anybody in their bed. In fact, the squeakings were specifically designed to be rather melodious and sound like nightingales. There was an intricate system of nails and brackets beneath each corridor, and even though the results were rather approximate, it was possible to imagine that there was an aviary of indignant birds beneath your feet. It's a clever and ancient form of the burglar alarm, and though the original Japanese *uguisu-bari* has never made it into English, *nightingale floor* has an entry all to itself in the OED. The other peculiar thing is that though the Japanese make them deliberately, in the West we have been accidentally making nightingale floors for ages. Rare and extremely new is the house where the floorboards don't sing like a violated canary, or where the door doesn't *screak* on its hinges – a splendidly jarring word that sounds like a combination of *scream* and *shriek*.

You may plan to be as *surrepent* (or creeping stealthily under-neath) as a *creep-mouse*, but you will probably sound more like a randy, post-ruminatory bull. The best you can do is, once beyond the nightingales, take Dr Johnson's advice and:

SOSS ... To fall at once into a chair.

Lamp-life

Before actually tottering *bedwards*, you may wish to get a few things done. After all, you may be *clinophobic* and have a mor-bid fear of going to bed. You could, as the expression has it, get next week's drinking done early, although considering what happened a couple of chapters ago I cannot recommend this. Or you could take this opportunity to get some work done.

Winston Churchill was the grand old master of working at odd hours of the day. His brain seemed to rise with the bull, and there are numerous stories of how he won the Second World War at times of day when most of us are tucked up and dreaming. He used to hold cabinet meetings at just around this time, which were known to the poor people who had to attend as Churchill's *midnight follies*. Then he would pace around the cabinet war rooms during the small hours phoning people up and giving orders that were often complete nonsense and rightly ignored. Alan Brooke, Churchill's Chief of Staff, later recalled that 'Winston had ten ideas every day, only one of which was good, and he didn't know which one it was'.[2]

Those who feel philogrobolized all morning, so-so in the afternoon, and decent in the evening, but who are only truly awake after midnight are called *lychnobites*. Lychnobite comes from the Greek *lychno-bios* and means, approximately, 'lamp-life' (that's the same *bio* that you get in *biology*, 'the study of life'). The word was invented by Seneca, but found its way into the English language in the early eighteenth century.

If you are a hard-working lychnobite, like Churchill, or if you are a lazy lychnobite who simply failed to get anything done in the day, like me, now is the time to *lucubrate*. Lucubrate means to work by lamp-light, and is quite the most civilised form of working there is. There is nobody around to tell you how to do things, or how fast to do things, or that you can't do things with your feet up and a little whisky. This is especially true if you have a good strong lock on your *lucubatory*.

A lucubatory is 'a place of midnight study', a room that you work in when all the world is sleeping around you. They are

---

[2] Churchill's chief military assistant, Hastings Ismay, estimated that the numbers were in fact twenty ideas a day with five good.

very hard to find and rarely mentioned in estate agents' par-
ticulars. Some people like to add extensions to their houses – a
games room, a gym, a private cinema – but if I ever have the
money I shall add a lucubatory. I feel sure that it would increase
my productivity no end, even though I would, of course, never
go in there until I had heard the chimes at midnight. For the
day, I would content myself with a *phrontistery*, which is 'a place
for thinking'. There the eager phrontist can muse and ponder,
ponder and muse to their heart's content, in a way that is utterly
impossible in a utility room. Descartes, incidentally, had a
phrontistery. He claimed to do all his best thinking sitting inside
a stove. Not while it was lit, of course, that would be uncomfortable. But perhaps that would be the ideal lucubatory: a stove by
day, and at night, when the embers have been raked out, a place
of meditation and sooty solitude.

Dr Johnson didn't work late at night, and referred to lucu-
braters as *candle-wasters*, which is cruel. But perhaps he was
right, and it is indeed time to *couch a hog's head*, *hit the hay*, and
head up the weary wooden hill to Bedfordshire.

Disrobing

Apodysophilia is 'a feverish desire to undress'. It is usually a term
of criminal psychology applied to people who do it in inappropriate places and get into trouble. The only appropriate places
for an attack of apodysophilia are the *apodyterium*, or undressing room, of a Roman bathhouse, and your own bedroom.

Here you may play the *ecdysiast* at will – ecdysiast being
a very learned term for a strip-tease artist invented by the

American satirist H.L. Mencken. He had received a letter from a lady called Georgia Southern, a distinguished stripper of the 1940s, who didn't like being called a stripper. She observed in her letter that:

> Strip-teasing is a formal and rhythmic disrobing of the body in public. In recent years there has been a great deal of uninformed criticism levelled against my profession. Most of it is without foundation and arises because of the unfortunate word strip-teasing, which creates the wrong connotations in the mind of the public. I feel sure that if you could coin a new and more palatable word to describe this art, the objections to it would vanish and I and my colleagues would have easier going.

H.L. Mencken, being a perfect gentleman, set himself to the task and eventually replied thus:

> I need not tell you that I sympathize with you in your affliction, and wish that I could help you. Unfortunately, no really persuasive new name suggests itself. It might be a good idea to relate strip-teasing in some way or other to the associated zoological phenomenon of molting. Thus the word moltician comes to mind, but it must be rejected because of its likeness to mortician. A resort to the scientific name for molting, which is ecdysis, produces both ecdysist and ecdysiast.

And ecdysiast it was. The term was instantly put to use by her publicist, got itself into the OED and even gave birth to the word *ecdysiasm* or 'the activity and occupation of strip teasing'.

You are nearly ready to leap into bed. First you must take your shoes off (a detail often omitted by ecdysiasts), which is technically noted as *discalcing*.

Finally, it is vital to check for *snudges*.

> Snudge, c. one that lurks under a bed, to watch an opportunity to Rob the House. (1699)

So down on your knees and have a good peek. There should be nothing down there except ...

> BEGGAR'S VELVET, s. the lightest particles of down shaken from a feather-bed, and left by a sluttish housemaid to collect under the bed till it covers the floor for want of due sweeping, and she gets a scolding from her dame.

So it's time to get into bed – and, speaking of scolding, there is a risk that that is what you are now to receive.

Domestic dragons

As noted in the Preambulation, I have never been quite sure in this book whether you are married or not. I observed a couple of chapters ago that I feared the worst, but just to interpose a little ease, let our frail thoughts dally with false surmise and assume that you are possessed of a top-of-the-line, state-of-the-art spouse. In which case, I don't see why you haven't got to bed until this extraordinary late hour. And nor does your spouse.

The relevant word here is *dragonism*. Dragons, quite aside from their wings and halitosis, have the extraordinary quality of never going to sleep. Instead, they are eternally watchful, guarding their treasure and fair maidens. Thus dragonism is the practice of staying awake for ever, ready to attack. Prepare for a lecture.

> **Curtain Lecture** A woman who scolds her husband when in
> bed, is said to read him a curtain lecture.

The idea here is that you sleep in a four-poster bed and it's only once the curtains are drawn around you that your spouse, be they male or female, starts confessing your faults. The curtains stop the sound travelling too far, and also protect you from observation if you are *gymnologising*, or 'having an argument in the nude', as the ancient Greeks often did.

The ancient Greeks were masters of argument and spent a lot of time classifying methods of making yourself look good and your opponent look bad. They called this rhetoric. There are precisely a million and one rhetorical forms, but two of them are surprisingly common, almost universal, in a good domestic set-to.

Paralipsis is the practice of mentioning that you're not mentioning something, and saying what you're not saying. That may sound like a strange and preposterous paradox, but consider the following:

> I'm not going to bring up how you were late, late by half an
> hour. And I'm not going to mention how you disgraced yourself

> at Percy's funeral, and I'm not even going to say a thing about
> your obsession with ferrets. All I'm saying is …

Do you see how it's done? You make a big show of saying what you're not saying. You list all the topics that you will not bring up. Now you know what paralipsis is – I am sure that you have used it yourself and had it used on you. It is the single most common rhetorical trope deployed in family rows. Any clause that begins with the words 'Not to mention' is paralipsis. Needless to say, it's a very clever technique because it allows you to score point after point without even allowing for a reply.

Epitrope is the granting of ironic permission, usually while listing all of the concomitant disadvantages. Consider the following:

> Go right ahead. Don't mind me. Really, don't. Stay out late.
> Ruin your liver. It doesn't bother me that you're heading for an
> early grave and I'm going to be left bankrupt and alone with
> seventeen children and a wooden leg. Why should that bother
> me? You just do what you want to do.

Familiar? The only advantage of epitrope is that it usually means you're somewhere near the end of the curtain lecture. If you're not, you may become *fugacious* or ready to run away from home.

If you're lucky, your curtain lecture may be *subderiserous*, or gently mocking. And if you are truly blessed, you may receive *levament*, which Dr Johnson defined as 'The comfort that one hath of his wife'.

Lying down to sleep

Night-spel, was a Prayer against the Night-mar. (1674)

Finally, your *Scotch warming pan* has ceased to scold you (mind you, it might all start up again if you call them a Scotch warming pan). It is time to put out the lights and *dowse the glims*, as a highwayman would have said. Highwaymen could never say anything in ordinary English, and they would bid you good night by saying *bene darkmans*, pronounced *BEN-ay*, and deriving from the Latin for blessed. So if there is somebody with you, that is how to wish them good night.

Wrap yourself up in the *panes* and *counterpanes*. A dictionary of eighteenth-century dialect words defines *healing* as 'covering with the bed-cloaths', and it can often feel like that. Heal yourself among the lily-white sheets, say a night-spell to protect you from nightmares and, if you like, hold a quick *couchée* where all your courtiers come and pay homage to you as you lie in bed at night.

When the last courtier has departed and you are left silent in your *dreamery* (a place that favours dreams), your *consopiation* (or 'act of laying to sleep') may start. The Sandman, Morpheus, Billy Winks and all the other gods of sleep will approach; and soon a Norfolk farmer of the eighteenth century will appear and tell you that you *dream drumbles*, which is only his way of saying that you are half asleep.

Then, as you are half-dreaming, there is a little twitch known as a *myoclonic jerk*, which sounds like a spicy Jamaican sauce but is only your body shifting with your dreams. And then you are asleep, and nothing is moving but that strange 'nocturnal spirit' found only in Dr Johnson's dictionary, the Ponk.

Epilogue

Well that's it, I suppose. It's over. The ploughman homeward drops into the western bay and all that. I am feeling *finifugal*, and I have to say goodbye to my dictionaries.

It's nearly closing time at the British Library anyway. Seven minutes left, by my watch. There are only two of us left in Rare Books and Music, and I think the other fellow may be dead: at least he hasn't moved in the last twenty minutes. And when they close, I'll have to hand in all my dictionaries and they'll go back to the vaults and sleep again.

Every dictionary contains a world. I open a book of thieves' slang from Queen Anne's reign and they have a hundred words for swords, for wenches, and for being hanged. They did not die, they *danced on nothing*. Then I peek into any one of my rural Victorian dictionaries, compiled by a lonely clergyman, with words for coppices, thickets, lanes, diseases of horses and innumerable terms for kinds of eel. They gave names to the things of their lives, and their lives are collected in these dictionaries – every detail and joke and belief. I have their worlds piled up on my desk.

And the highwaymen are all hanged, the farmers are gone under their earth, and the RAF pilots who called the North Sea the *Juice*, the Atlantic the *Pond*, and the English Channel the *Drink* are lying at the bottom of all three.

All these worlds are departed, dead and dancing on nothing. They will not come back, but they are here in these books that I must hand in to the lady at the desk. It doesn't do to spend too

long with dictionaries, or I'll end up like Lot's beloved: salsicolumnified, gazing on my lost Gomorrahs.

That's it. The librarians are dowsing the glims, and even the
dead chap's getting up to leave. I shall return my dictionaries.
Bene darkmans, sleeping reader, bene darkmans.

Paralipomenon
– The Drinker's Dictionary

Here is that list of Benjamin Franklin's terms for drunkenness in full:

The Drinker's Dictionary

He's addled, in his airs, affected, casting up his accounts, biggy, bewitched, black and black, bowzed, boozy, been at Barbadoes, been watering the brook, drunk as a wheelbarrow, bothered, burdocked, bosky, busky, buzzy, has sold a march in the brewer, has a head full of bees, has been in the bibing plot, has drunk more than he has bled, is bungy, has been playing beggar-my-neighbour, drunk as a beggar, sees the beams, has kissed black Betty, has had a thump over the head with Samson's jaw-bone, has been at war with his brains, is bridgy, has been catching the cat, is cogniaid, capable, cramped, cherubimical, cherry merry, wamble croft, cracked, half way to Concord, canon-ized, has taken a chirping glass, got corns in his head, got a cup too much, coguay, cupsy, has heated his copper, is in crocus, catched, cuts capers, has been in the cellar, been in the sun, is in his cups, above the clouds, is non compos, cocked, curved, cut, chippered, chickenny, has loaded his cart, been too free with the creature. Sir Richard has taken off his considering cap, he's chopfallen, candid, disguised, got a dish, has killed a dog, has taken his drops. 'Tis a dark day with him. He's a dead man, has dipped his bill, sees double, is disfigured, has seen the devil, is prince Eugene, has entered, buttered both eyes, is cock-eyed, has got the pole evil, has got a brass eye, has made an example, has ate a toad and a half for breakfast, is in his element, is fishy, foxed, fuddled, soon fuddled, frozen, will have frogs for supper, is well in front, is getting forward in the world, owes no man money, fears no man, is crump fooled, has been to France, is flushed, has frozen his mouth, is fettered, has been to a funeral, has his flag out, is fuzzled, has spoken with his friend, been at an Indian feast, is glad, grabable, great-headed, glazed, generous, has boozed the gage, is as dizzy as a goose, has been before George, got the gout, got a kick in the guts, been at Geneva, is globular, has got the glanders, is on the go, a gone man, has been to see Robin Goodfellow, is half and half, half seas over, hardy, top heavy, has got by the head, makes head way, is hiddey, has got on his little hat, is hammerish, loose in the hilt, knows not the way home, is haunted by evil spirits, has taken Hippocrates' grand Elixir, is intoxicated, jolly, jagged, jambled, jocular, juicy, going to Jericho, an indirect man, going to Jamaica, going to Jerusalem, is a king, clips the King's English, has seen the French king. The King is his cousin, has got kibed heels, has got knapt, his kettle's hot. He'll soon keel upward, he's in his liquor, lordly, light, lappy, limber, lopsided, makes indentures with his legs, is well to live, sees two moons, is merry, middling, muddled, moon-eyed, maudlin, mountainous, muddy, mellow, has seen a flock of moons, has raised his monuments, has eaten cacao nuts, is nimtopsical, has got the night mare, has been nonsuited, is super nonsensical, in a state of nature, nonplussed, oiled, has ate opium, has smelt an onion, is an oxycrocum, is overset, overcome, out of sorts, on the paymaster's books, drank his last halfpenny, is as good conditioned as a puppy, is pigeon eyed, pungy, priddy, pushing on, has salt in his headban, has been among the Philistines, is in prosperity, is friends with Philip, contending with Pharaoh, has painted his nose, wasted his punch, learned politeness, eat the pudding-bag, eat too much pumpkin, is full of piety, is rocky, raddled, rich, religious, ragged, raised, has lost his rudder, has been too far with Sir Richard, is like a rat in trouble, is stitched, seafaring, in the suds, strong, as drunk as David's sow, swamped, his skin is full, steady, stiff, burnt his shoulder, has got out his topgallant sails, seen the dog-star, is stiff as a ringbolt. The shoe pinches him. He's staggerish. It is star light with him. He carries too much sail, will soon out studding sails, is stewed, stubbed, soaked, soft, has made too free with Sir John Strawberry, right before the wind, all sails out, has pawned his senses, plays parrot, has made shift of his shirt, shines like a blanket, has been paying for a sign, is toped, tongue-tied, tanned, tipsicum grave, double tongued, tospey turvey, tipsy, thawed, trammulled, transported, has swallowed a tavern token, makes Virginia fame, has got the Indian vapours, is pot valiant, in love with varany, wise, has a wet soul, has been to the salt water, in search of eye water, is in the way to be weaned, out of the way, water soaked, wise or otherwise, can walk the line. The wind is west with him. He carries the wagon.

Dictionaries and Idioticons

(An *idioticon* is a dictionary of a particular dialect
or area of language)

Abedecarium Anglico-Latinum, Richard Huloet (1552)

Worlde of Wordes, John Florio (1598)

*A Table Alphabeticall, conteyning the true writing and
understanding of hard usual English wordes, borrowed from
the Hebrew, Greeke, Latine, or French. &c.*, Robert Cawdrey
(1604)

*A New Dictionary of the Terms Ancient and Modern of the
Canting Crew*, B.E. Gent. (1699)

*Glossographia Anglicana nova: or, a dictionary, interpreting such
hard words of whatever language, as are at present used in
the English tongue, with their etymologies, definitions, &c.*,
Thomas Blount (1656)

An Universal Etymological Dictionary, Nathan Bailey (1721)

Dictionary of the English Language, Samuel Johnson (1755)

Sports and Pastimes of the People of England, Joseph Strutt
(1801), enlarged by Charles Cox (1903)

An Etymological Dictionary of the Scottish Language, Reverend
John Jamieson (1808)

A Classical Dictionary of the Vulgar Tongue, Francis Grose etc. (1811). Grose died in 1791 but his dictionary continued to be expanded (and occasionally contracted) for a couple of decades after his death. I have used whatever edition I found most amusing.

The Vocabulary of East Anglia; An Attempt to Record the Vulgar Tongue of the Twin Sister Counties, Norfolk and Suffolk as It Existed In the Last Years of the Eighteenth Century, and Still Exists, Reverend Robert Forby (1830)

Westmoreland and Cumberland dialects: Dialogues, poems, songs, and ballads, John Russell Smith (1839)

A Pentaglot Dictionary of the Terms Employed in Anatomy, Physiology, Pathology, Practical Medicine, Surgery, Obstetrics, Medical Jurisprudence, Materia Medica, Pharmacy, Medical Zoology, Botany and Chemistry, Shirley Palmer (1845)

Dictionary of Obsolete and Provincial English, Thomas Wright (1857)

A Dictionary of Modern, Slang, Cant, and Vulgar Words Used at the Present Day in the Streets of London, John Camden Hotten (1860)

The Dialect of Leeds and its Neighbourhood Illustrated by Conversations and Tales of Common Life etc., C. Clough Robinson (1862)

A Dictionary of the Terms Used in Medicine and the Collateral Sciences, Richard D. Hoblyn (1865)

A glossary of words used in the wapentakes of Manley and Corringham, Lincolnshire, Edward Peacock (1877)

Shropshire word-book, a glossary of archaic and provincial words, &c., used in the county, Georgina Jackson (1879)

Slang and its Analogues, John Stephen Farmer (1893)

English Dialect Dictionary, Joseph Wright (1898–1905)

A Scots Dialect Dictionary, Alexander Warrack (1911)

Western Canadian dictionary and phrase-book: things a newcomer wants to know, John Sandilands (1912)

Cab Calloway's Hepsters Dictionary: Language of Jive, Cabell Calloway (1938–44)

Psychiatric Dictionary with Encyclopaedic Treatment of Modern Terms, Leland Earl Hinsie (1940)

Service Slang, J.L. Hunt and A.G. Pringle, Faber (1943)

Dictionary of Guided Missiles and Space Flight, Grayson Merrill (1959)

A Descriptive Dictionary and Atlas of Sexology, ed. Robert T. Francoeur, Greenwood (1991). N.B. This book does actually contain maps, although the term 'atlas' may be overstating it a bit.

Straight from the Fridge, Dad: A Dictionary of Hipster Slang (3rd edition), No Exit Press (2004)

Fubar: Soldier Slang of World War II, Gordon L. Rottman, Osprey (2007)

Chambers Slang Dictionary, Jonathon Green (2008)

The Oxford English Dictionary, OUP (2012)

*

However, a few words were not in any of these dictionaries:

Dysania is in use as a technical medical term (see, for example, *Myalgic Encephalomyelitis: A Baffling Syndrome with a Tragic Aftermath*, Ramsay, 1989) and also makes a show in a medical word-finder of 1958 called the *Reversicon*. But I've never found it in what I'd call a dictionary.

Groke is, or was, a Scottish dialect word mentioned in *History of the European Languages or, Researches into the Affinities of the Teutonic, Greek, Celtic, Sclavonic and Indian Nations* (1823) by Alexander Murray, who was Professor of Oriental Languages at the University of Edinburgh; he applied it exclusively to dogs.

Nooningscaup appears in *Clavis Calendaria* by John Henry Brady (1812), who mentions it as a contemporary term in Yorkshire.

The citation of *gongoozler* is from the 'Glossary of Canal Terms' skulking at the back of *Bradshaw's Canals and Navigable Rivers of England and Wales* by Henry Rodolph de Salis (1918).

The keys to the indoor tank park comes from my vast network of spies within the British army.

I was introduced to the term *gabos* by a Special Adviser to Her Majesty's Government who said it was commonly used round their way. I've since found various references to it on the Internet and one in a documentary that pins it down as a Miami criminal term. To my knowledge it has never made it into any print dictionary and has no currency outside of the Miami Mega Max Jail facility and the Palace of Westminster.

The tasseographical terms were culled from *Tea-Cup Reading and the Art of Fortune Telling by Tea-Leaves* by 'A Highland Seer', The Musson Book Co., Toronto (1920).

Shturmovshchina is a Russian term that has never made it into an English dictionary. However, it was much too delightful a word to exclude.

The definition of *cinqasept* is from *The Oxford Essential Dictionary of Foreign Terms in English*, ed. Jennifer Speake, Berkley Books (1999). I'm particularly fond of the idea that an afternoon visit to one's mistress could qualify as *Essential*.

Several of the terms in the shopping section do not appear in dictionaries. They were instead gleaned from people who work in the British retail trade.

The term 'drunk as four hundred rabbits' is mentioned in *México* by William Weber Johnson (1966). The Centzon Totochtin, from which the phrase must derive, are a standard part of Aztec mythology.

The definition of *smikker* comes from *A Chronicle of Scottish Poetry; From the Thirteenth Century to the Union of the Crowns: to which is added a Glossary*, J. Sibbald (1802).

There is also one word (quite aside from salsicolumnified) that I made up off the top of my head. But unless you check every word in this book against all the dictionaries listed above, you'll never find it. If you *do* check all the words in this book against all those dictionaries, I have nothing for you but my pity, and my curse.

Index

Chapter 18: 11 p.m.

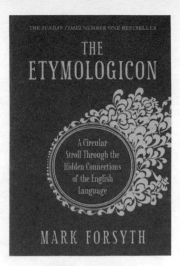

also available:

The Etymologicon

A Circular Stroll Through the Hidden Connections
of the English Language

The *Sunday Times* Number One Bestseller

'I'm hooked on Forsyth's book ... Crikey, but this is addictive'
—Matthew Parris, *The Times*

What is the actual connection between *disgruntled* and *gruntled*?
What links church organs to organised crime, California to the
Caliphate, or brackets to codpieces?

As heard on BBC Radio 4, *The Etymologicon* – which springs
from Mark Forsyth's Inky Fool blog – is an occasionally ribald,
frequently witty and unerringly erudite guided tour of the
secret labyrinth that lurks beneath the English language. It takes
in monks and monkeys, film buffs and buffaloes, and explains
precisely what the Rolling Stones have to do with gardening.

ISBN 978-184831-453-5

£8.99

The Etymologicon

– the unabridged audiobook read by
Simon Shepherd – is published
by AudioGO (9781445847429)
and available now from
audiogo.co.uk